A Companion Guide to
Bush Food

A Companion Guide to
Bush Food

Jennifer Isaacs

LANSDOWNE

Distributed by Gary Allen Pty Ltd
9 Cooper Street, Smithfield, NSW 2164
Published by Lansdowne Publishing Pty Ltd
Level 5, 70 George Street, Sydney NSW 2000, Australia

Chief Executive Publisher: Jane Curry
Production Manager: Sally Stokes
Publishing Manager: Cheryl Hingley

First published 1996

Edited by Cynthia Blanche
Designed by Avenir Design
Printed by South China Printing Company, Hong Kong

© Copyright: Jennifer Isaacs 1996
© Copyright Design: Lansdowne Publishing 1996

ISBN 1 86302 514 6

All rights reserved. Subject to the Copyright Act 1968, no part of this publication may be reproduced, stored in a retrieval system, or transmitted in any form, or by any means, electronic, mechanical, photocopying, recording, or otherwise, without the prior written permission of the publisher.

Cover photograph by Leo Meier

CONTENTS

Introduction 7

Bush Foods,
listed alphabetically
by common name 8

Index 150

INTRODUCTION

This *Companion Guide to Bush Food* has been distilled from the larger work *Bush Food: Aboriginal Food and Herbal Medicine*, to enable easy use when travelling. The foods covered are in the main still gathered, processed and eaten by Aboriginal families who enjoy bush food and prefer to live close to their land.

Before Europeans came to Australia over 200 years ago, the country sustained hundreds of thousands (some say up to one million) Aborigines. Although there were many different languages and cultures throughout the country, strict rules governed food and plant harvesting. Areas of land were owned, and still are, by kinship groups, and people, plants and animals are still linked by religious beliefs from the Dreaming when fruits and food were created by the Ancestral Spirits. Foods were gathered only when seasonal indicators were just right — when a particular tree flowered or the winds changed. These lessons are still relevant today, as some bush foods are quite inedible when under-ripe and others require specialised processing to remove toxins. I will always value greatly the sharing of this knowledge with me over many years.

The Companion is designed as a guide to understanding and observing nature and to be used as an adjunct to informed bush and outback travelling in Australia.

In Arnhem Land vegetables and meat are wrapped in paperbark and cooked in a ground oven. PHOTO: LEO MEIER

A

ALEXANDER PALM

Gronophyllum ramsayi

Aborigines collect the heart of this palm – known as *bulmurrk* – in monsoon jungle areas from Yirrkala to western Arnhem Land.

The trunk is severed about half a metre from the ground and the leaves and outer pith cut off. The central core of the trunk is exposed and cut into sections. The pithy end is discarded but the middle core or heart of the palm is eaten on the spot by all present. Children in particular love this fresh delicious vegetable and munch it like an apple.

ANTS see GREEN ANTS, HONEY ANTS

APPLE BERRY

Billardiera scandens

This is one of the many twining climbers of the southeastern states that have edible fruit. It grows in forests and bears cream tubular flowers followed by fleshy edible fruits up to 2 centimetres long. The cylindrical berries are green or yellow, holding many small seeds in a sweet pulp. As the fruit ripens it falls from the bush, so that edible fruit is mostly found on the ground.

*Apple berries (*Billardiera scandens*) grow freely in open woodlands of southeastern Australia. If gathered when they drop from the vine, they are sweet and palatable.*
PHOTO: JENNIFER ISAACS

*Apple berries (*Billardiera scandens*). The over-ripe fruit is sweet tasting.*
PHOTO: JENNIFER ISAACS

BAOBAB NUT

Adansonia gregorii

This tree is usually called boab tree in the Kimberley region of Western Australia. It is distinctive for its huge bulbous trunk and large 'nuts' the size of emu eggs. The nuts must be harvested when mature but before they become hard.

The seeds and pith are eaten by Aborigines either raw or after being dipped in water, sweetened with honey. Old reports say that the seeds and pith were also pounded and cooked into bread. The dry pith tastes like sherbet.

BIRDS see GEESE, DUCKS ETC.

BLACK BEAN; MORETON BAY CHESTNUT

Castanospermum australe

The Moreton Bay chestnut tree bears large seeds that are processed to yield a saponin-free flour. The trees are found in Queensland rainforests and, though not relished, provide some protein, fat and fibre in the traditional Aboriginal diet. The nuts are leached thoroughly to remove toxins, then pounded and made into cakes, after which they are roasted.

The distinctive boab tree of Western Australia bears huge nuts the size of emu eggs which contain a pithy substance tasting like sherbert. PHOTO: JENNIFER ISSACS

Boab nuts are engraved with totemic animals and designs and, when dry, are used as rattles for dances. PHOTO: REG MORRISON

*Moreton Bay chestnuts (*Castanospermum australe*). These must be roasted, sliced and leached thoroughly to remove toxins before being eaten.* PHOTO: VIC CHERIKOFF

BLACK FRUIT

Terminalia muellen; T. melanocarpa

Black fruit are found all over Cape York, most frequently along the northern beaches of Cairns. The tree bears many small blue-black fruit about the size of a fingernail. Black fruit appear at the height of the monsoon period when vegetables and fruits are hard to find. Before the advent of store goods, they provided a welcome if small source of fresh fruit.

BLACK NERITES

Nerita lineata

These shellfish, called *drangol* in Cape York, live on the lower branching above-ground roots of mangrove trees. Although small, they are quite delicious, rather like periwinkles.

These shells are usually boiled. To remove the flesh a pin or strong, sharp fishbone is hooked into the flesh at the opening and the pin and shell are rotated in opposite directions so that the flesh comes out (one hopes) in a complete spiral. Black nerites are never a staple food but add variety to the diet.

Small black nerites, known as drangol, *cling to the mangrove roots.*
PHOTO: JENNIFER ISAACS

BOGONG MOTHS
Agrotis infusa

Any account of Aboriginal harvesting of edible grubs and insects would not be complete without mentioning the extraordinary moth feasts that once occurred in the Bogong mountains of southern New South Wales. The Omeo-Monaro tribes of the Bogong country are now fewer in number and the moths remain unmolested, aestivating in millions every year in the same rock shelters of the mountains where hundreds of people once gathered and grew fat on their nutritious bodies.

From November to January up to seven hundred people from different tribes would assemble for huge feasts on the moths, *Agrotis infusa*, which could be found sheltering in the recesses of rocks and in caves. The stone surface of every crevice was covered with a layer of tightly packed moths. Aborigines collected moths by dislodging the bottom row with a stick and

Bogong moths aestivate in great numbers in the colder mountainous areas of Canberra and southern New South Wales.

PHOTO: VIC CHERIKOFF

catching them as they fell on a kangaroo skin or a specially woven fibre cloth placed on the floor of the cave or on the ground below the rock. They cooked the moths by rolling them lightly in hot ashes and sifting the bodies gently in a string bag to separate the wings and heads from the bodies. The resulting mass of flesh was very small; one writer described it as the size a grain of wheat after cooking. Occasionally the moths were pounded up and made into a form of cake that apparently could be kept for a few days. The early literature described the moths as being extremely 'nice and sweet, with the flavour of walnut'.

BRACKEN

Pteridum esculentum

The common bracken fern has become a pest in some country areas and is often the first plant to regenerate after fire. The thin, starchy rhizomes are edible from late summer to autumn, but must be processed to avoid possible ill effects. Some Aborigines pounded the rhizomes to extract the starch, which is cooked in cakes as the rhizomes alone are very fibrous.

BUFFALO *see* INTRODUCED GAME

BULRUSH

Typha spp.

Common bulrushes grow in shallow water of creeks, rivers and swamps. The bulrush is an easily recognised aquatic plant as it has a flower spike shaped like a brown rod protruding well above the

*Bulrushes (*Typha *sp.). The new white shoots of these common aquatic plants are edible.* PHOTO: DIANA CONROY

water. The rush grows prolifically in warmer months, reaching a height of 2.5 metres.

The very new white to green shoots of these rushes are gathered and eaten raw or cooked by Aborigines of the marshlands of south western Australia and the Murray-Darling system of New South Wales.

The glutinous rhizome was roasted and provided starch, sugar and a considerable amount of fibre to the people of Victoria and New South Wales. According to the explorer Thomas Mitchell, bulrushes were the principal food of Aborigines of the Lachlan River. He observed them wading through the swamps gathering large bundles and carrying them in net bags on their heads.

BUNYA PINE
Araucaria bidwillii

The bunya pine is an enormously tall tree, up to 80 metres high, from the mountains of southeastern Queensland and northern New South Wales. It bears huge cones full of nuts. Although they fruit each year, they are particularly plentiful every three years. In the past, up to three hundred Aborigines gathered from different tribes to feast on the nuts. Descriptions of the bunya feasts are in many ways similar to those of the bogong moth gatherings of the alpine area in that observers described the Aborigines as living on a diet of nuts and emerging from the feasts and ceremonies 'sleek and fat'. Constance Petrie in her book about her father's memories, *Tom Petrie's Reminiscences*, says that the pine is wrongly pronounced 'bunya'. It should be

Almond-shaped nuts of the bunya bunya pine and Moreton Bay chestnuts. Bunya nuts are delicious raw or roasted but Moreton Bay chestnuts require processing. PHOTO: DIANA CONROY
Overleaf: Bunya pines in Southern Queensland.

'bon-yi', the 'i' being sounded as an 'e' in English, which was the way the Aborigines used to pronounce it. Tom claims that his grandfather, Andrew Petrie, discovered the tree, but when he gave some specimens to a Mr Bidwill, who forwarded them to England for classification, the tree was inadvertently named after him.

The cones are gathered by a man slinging a vine around the trunk, tying the rest of the rope around his waist and hoisting his body upward by clinging to the tree with his feet. Notches are sometimes cut into the tree trunks to help the

18 BUNYA PINE

ascent. The nuts are eaten both raw and cooked and were feasted upon until the season was over. The gatherings to feast on bunya nuts were times for ceremonial exchange, when different communities coming together would pass on songs and dances. These great ceremonies, which culminated when a particular food supply was plentiful in one area, were the means by which rituals and song cycles were transmitted from one part of the country to another.

BURDEKIN PLUM

Pleiogynium timorense

This spreading tree of the mango family grows to 20 metres. The purple-black fruit are about 5 centimetres long, rather like small pumpkins. They are frequently seen growing in Brisbane gardens, and at Cairns and Yorkey's Knob. The fruit is edible only when completely ripe and even better when kept for a few days after picking. Aborigines buried it in sand for up to two weeks before eating it.

BURRAWANG NUTS

Macrozamia spiralis; M. miquelii; M. communis

The dwarf zamia palm, found in the forests of southeast Australia, has fruit somewhat like a pineapple. The seeds or nuts were eaten after leaching and cooking.

A small group of zamias occurs in the Macdonnell Ranges in central Australia (*Macrozamia macdonnellii*). These are the only cycads which were not eaten by Aborigines.

Brilliantly coloured zamiad nuts form a pineapple-shaped cone.
PHOTO: VIC CHERIKOFF

Cycads and zamias contain toxins which cause nerve damage after prolonged eating and inadequate processing. In cattle this is known as the 'zamiad staggers'.

BUSH CARROT

Abelmoschus moschatus

This small pointed tuber looks like a miniature parsnip and tastes like a carrot, hence its colloquial name. In the Djinang language of central Arnhem Land it is called *marrakangalay*. Although infrequently eaten, it is nevertheless admired for its taste after being cooked in the ashes or, with other vegetables and yams, in a ground oven.

*Bush carrot (*Abelmoschus moschatus*) of central Arnhem Land.*
PHOTO: LEO MEIER

BUSH CASHEW NUT

Semicarpus australiensis

Called *ganyawu* in eastern Arnhem Land, these nuts grow on large shade trees of the Arnhem Land forests. The sap is very irritant and Aborigines prevent their children climbing up the trunk and branches as the skin can develop allergic itchy patches on contact.

The nuts are attached to hard, yellow jelly-like matter, which must be removed and safely discarded away from children. They are encased in a 'skin' that is also poisonous and must be burnt off.

Mothers have to wash their hands carefully after preparing *ganyawu* before they touch their babies. The traditional way is to rub them with cuttlefish and water, then rub some passionfruit leaves into a lather and use it as soap.

BUSH ONIONS

Cyperus bulbosus

This is a small onion sedge with corms on shallow roots the size of shallots. To the Warlpiri it is known as *janmarda*; to the Arrente, *yelka*; and to the Pitjantjatjara it is *nyiri*. Eaten raw or cooked, the corms may be kept for a period in underground storage. They have a tough husk that is removed before eating. In some areas the corms are placed on flat ground and spinifex is burned over them until the corms crack. Sometimes they are put in hot sand and the husks rubbed until the skin cracks. When the rains come all underground

Opposite: Davidson plums, brown pine plum, lillypilly and red monkey nuts. Semitropical and temperate Australian bush fruits and nuts are grown widely in parks and gardens. PHOTO: LEO MEIER

Bush onions, or yelka, (Cyperus bulbosus) may be eaten raw or cooked after removing the hard casing.
PHOTO: HAROLD WELDON

vegetables begin to shoot and are not harvested again until a month or so after the rains have ended and the tubers have matured. Women say the onions are not good to eat when they are in the early growing phase after rain.

This tasty bulb is interesting in that the Pitjantjatjara have named paper and books *nyiri* because of paper's resemblance to the skin of the onion bulb. It has a high water content, good protein levels and some fat and trace elements.

BUSH POTATO

Vigna lanceolata

Among the Guparbingu people of central Arnhem Land, the *limbuk* or *gingin* are cooked in the ashes all year round. This small, thin tuber has a sweet potato-like flavour. The plant has oval leaves in clumps of three.

Vigna species are also commonly eaten yams of the central desert regions. Here, the species is a low-growing plant that favours fine, relatively moist sediments, often occurring along watercourses. It has a thin taproot up to 20 centimetres in length, eaten raw or roasted. Food analysis shows it to have a high water content, some protein and carbohydrate and many trace elements, like the cultivated sweet potato.

Limbuk *or* gingin, *the bush potato (* Vigna lanceolata*) of central Arnhem Land.*
PHOTO: LEO MEIER

BUSH TOMATOES, RAISINS, SULTANAS

Solanum spp.

Sultana	*yakajiri*	*Solanum ellipticum*
Raisin	*kampurarpa*	*S. centrale*
Green tomato	*wanakidji*	*S. chippendalei*
Green tomato	*ngaru*	*S. petrophilum*
Yellow fruit	*albaraji*	*S. cleistogamum*
	yipirntiri	*S. cleistogamum*
Yellow fruit	*(southeast Australia)*	*S. esuriale*

The many species of solanum are related to the 'deadly' nightshade and some contain the toxic alkaloid solanine, which is found in green potatoes (also of the nightshade family). Some solanums are extremely important desert staples. Care must be taken before eating solanums as they can be highly toxic.

Two species of solanum are commonly eaten by the Pitjantjatjara people: *kampurarpa*, desert raisin (*Solanum centrale* or *S. ellipticum*) and *ngaru*, desert tomato, (*S. petrophilum*). When ripe the fruits of both these solanum species look like small green tomatoes; however, *ngaru* is slightly more bitter. The advantage of these fruits to Aborigines is that they ripen at different times of the year – *ngaru* from December to January, and *kampurarpa* from July to August. *Ngaru* eventually rot on the bush, whereas *kampurarpa* dry on the bush and can be found at any time of the year looking like dried raisins. They are gathered both fresh and dry. *Ngaru* is simply picked ripe from the bush, but the *kampurarpa* bush is shaken until the fruit drops on to the ground. The *ngaru* must be cleaned of seeds and this is done with a small sharpened stick about 15 centimetres long, flattened like a spatula. A single deft wrist motion is enough to separate the fruit from the seed, leaving only the thin flesh and skin. Many *ngaru* skins are eaten on the hunt; others are brought back to camp.

The fruits of *Solanum centrale* are particularly prevalent after fire. These plants tend to grow in large numbers in confined and well-known areas that are 'looked after' by Aboriginal people, not only by firing but occasionally by damming watercourses after heavy rain so that the run-off services patches of fruiting vegetation. The various solanum fruits are still gathered by desert women whenever they move from base camp, though most, except for bush tomatoes, are now eaten during the foraging expedition, with only a few being brought back to camp.

In the more arid regions of Victoria, the yellow berries of a similar plant, *Solanum esuriale*, were eaten raw or cooked.

The solanum fruits so far analysed have good amounts of carbohydrate and varying amounts of protein, with vitamin C and thiamine.

Desert raisins and tomatoes of various Solanum varieties are extremely valuable staple foods.
PHOTO:
HAROLD WELDON

*Desert raisins or kampurarpa (*Solanum centrale*). These may be eaten as dried fruit or ground into a seedy paste, formed into balls and dried.*
PHOTO: REG MORRISON

*Pale violet flowers of the bush tomato (*Solanum chippendalei*).*
PHOTO: LEO MEIER

*Cherry ballart. This species is a yellow variety (*Exocarpus latifolius*).*
PHOTOS: VIC CHERLKOFF

CHERRY BALLART

Exocarpus cupressiformis

One of the most widely known Aboriginal fruits in southeast Australia is the cherry ballart, which derives its colloquial name from similar Aboriginal names given to the fruit – *ballee* and *ballat* in Gippsland, *pallert* at Lake Condah and *balad* as far south as Wilson's Promontory.

The tree occurs widely in eucalypt forests and grows between 3 and 7 metres high. Young trees resemble weeping cypress trees with thin, leafless branches that hang as the tree grows. The fruits are small and distinctive, each small seed being supported on a large, swollen fleshy stalk that appears itself to be the fruit. The fruits eventually turn deep red or pink, when they become sweet and palatable.

Exocarpus *sp.*
PHOTOS: VIC CHERLKOFF

COCKY APPLE; WILD QUINCE

Planchonia careya

These elegant trees are found throughout the open forests of Queensland and the Northern Territory. The trees bear huge quantities of long ovoid fruit, yellow to green when ripe and with a fleshy pulp over several seeds. Known as *jungara* or *dhangi* at Ramingining, the blossom-like flowers have numerous radiating stamens that are sometimes threaded on strings to make ornaments and personal decorations for young girls. Cocky apples taste a little like quinces.

Flower of the wild quince of the north, a large tree which bears numerous small fruit known as cocky apples.

PHOTO: LEO MEIER

CONVOLVULUS

Ipomoea spp.

The common native convolvulus is harvested by Aborigines for its edible taproot. The vines of a number of species bear distinctive purple, mauve or pink flowers and can be seen on beaches in all parts of Australia. The thick taproots of *Ipomoea gracilis* and *I. brasiliensis*, for example, are gathered and roasted in the hot ashes.

The roots of *I. graminea*, or grass-leaved convolvulus, are high in energy and water with good levels of carbohydrate and protein and some fat and trace elements.

Convolvulus. PHOTO: JENNIFER ISAACS

CORAL TREE
Erythrina vespertilio

The fibrous roots of the seedlings of the *ininti* tree, *Erythrina vespertilio*, are sometimes eaten by the Warlpiri, Pintubi, Alyawara and related groups of the desert. This large tree grows up to 10 metres high along desert water-courses.

Erythrina roots, along with other desert tubers such as *Leichhardtia australis*, *Clerodendrum floribundum* and *Boerhavia diffusa* are roasted, then scraped or pounded with rocks to separate the flesh from the fibrous inner core, which is discarded. Only the skin and flesh are eaten.

Erythrina or *ininti* trees are always pointed out by western desert women on bush food expeditions, not so much for the tubers of the saplings but for their bright red seeds. These are gathered and strung into necklaces, headbands and chest ornaments to be worn by women and children when dancing. The root is an occasional food only and is collected infrequently.

CRABS see MUD CRABS

CYCAD
Cycas armstrongii

Stands of cycads are found in the dry open woodland of northwest Australia, Cape York and Arnhem Land. They are low plants, each producing twenty to thirty large seeds that radiate on stalks beneath palm-like branches. They are easily harvested. Usually several women gather, crack and pound them as a communal activity. The cycads are particularly interesting in that their yield increases dramatically after fire and the practice of burning

Left: Arnhem Land cycad palms (Cycas armstrongii).
Below: Bunya nuts, macadamias and quandong seeds.
PHOTO: LEO MEIER

When ripe, the cycad nuts hang beneath the fronds and drop to the ground. Baked ceremonial cakes are made after pounding, leaching and fermenting the kernels of the toxic nuts.
PHOTO: JENNIFER ISAACS

off large areas of grassy woodland in Arnhem Land has ensured their large numbers. They are a favoured food because they can be stored.

The nuts are highly toxic in their unprocessed state. Virtually every group of explorers in Australia from the early nineteenth century onward suffered the effects of poisoning from eating the tempting nuts of the cycad tree. The nuts are also poisonous to cattle, which suffer a form of nervous disease called zamia staggers if they graze in cycad country. The toxin, macrozamin or cycasin, produces tumours of the liver, kidney, intestine and brain after a period of a year or more. Zamia staggers is associated with degeneration of the spinal cord. In humans, eating untreated cycad nuts causes such intense vomiting and diarrhoea, but it is virtually impossible to eat sufficient to produce zamia staggers. Cattle seem able to eat the food without immediate sickness and so the toxin can accumulate.

It is quite remarkable that Aborigines have developed the processing and cooking technology necessary to render the seeds of cycads edible. Cycads grow in groves and bear very large quantities of fruit: one report indicated that 13 kilograms could be gathered in a 10 x 20 metre plot.

The method of removing poison from cycads varies throughout the country, but generally involves pounding the nut kernels, soaking them for a considerable period in still or running water, then mashing the fermented nuts into a paste that is made into a damper and cooked in the ashes. In north Queensland and at Yirrkala the kernels are

34 CYCAD

Ancient cycad nut palms form an understorey in the schlerophyll forests of Arnhem Land. PHOTO: LEO MEIER

roughly pounded, dried for three to four hours in the sun and put in string bags in a running stream for four or five days, followed by still water for another three or four days. The nuts have then fermented into a bubbling, smelly mass. This is squeezed and compressed to remove the liquid, then pounded between stones and reduced to a paste. Each woman has her own special grinding stone for cycad nuts, often left at the grinding site until the next time the nuts are needed.

The paste that results from the grinding is extremely thick. It is wrapped in small bundles of paperbark bound with strips of pandanus. The parcels are cooked in a small depression scraped out beneath the hot ashes. The cycad meal cooks slowly. When ready, it is removed from the ashes and the paperbark is peeled back to reveal the food. Cycad bread can be kept for many months, but in central Arnhem Land must not be eaten by women or children unless the older men give their permission. It is a special food prepared by the women only for men participating in sacred ceremonies. No reports seem really sure just how the poison is destroyed during this cooking process, if indeed it is all destroyed.

Aboriginal people are highly aware of the poisonous nature of the cycad nut. During the dehusking process the women's hands become covered with a grey substance that has to be washed off periodically. Great care is always taken to ensure that it does not fall into any unattended cups of tea around the camp or contaminate drinking water.

DAVIDSON'S PLUM

Davidsonia pruriens

This small rainforest tree grows to 12 metres and has pinnate leaves with slightly irritant hairs and small flowers. The 5-centimetre-long plum-shaped fruits are purple on the outside, scarlet inside, and quite acidic. They are highly prized for jam.

DESERT BANANA

Leichhardtia australis

This variety of bush banana found in central Australia is called *yuparli* by Warlpiri people. The small vines climb young trees or grow in rock crevices close to dry riverbeds in spinifex country. The fruit resembles small dry chokos. The *yuparli* are cooked before eating if they are mature, though young pods are eaten raw along with flowers and leaves. The fire is scooped aside, exposing the dry ground beneath the ashes, and the bananas are baked together with other vegetables by covering

*The desert banana (*Leichhardtia australis*). Young green pods are eaten raw, along with flowers and leaves. Mature brown pods are roasted lightly under the coals and taste like a mixture of zucchini, pumpkin and beans.*
PHOTO: LEO MEIER

The edible fibrous interior of a cooked desert banana.
PHOTO: LEO MEIER

them with coals. They taste somewhat like stringy zucchini with echoes of pumpkin and beans. The green flesh is eaten as well as the seedy pulpy centre, which lifts out intact when cooked. When raw, the inside looks like kapok.

DESERT SEED DAMPER

For the Pitjantjatjara women, several seeds provided the basis of different breads. The portulaca plant, known as *wakati* to the Pitjantjatjara, as well as various grasses, in particular *Panicum* species, were considered to be delicious seed for bread.

Recipes for damper and Johnny cakes have appeared in colonial cookbooks since the earliest days of European settlement. It is still true that damper, preferably with some bush honey (replaced with golden syrup by the newcomers) and billy tea offers the archetypal Australian bush meal for Aborigines and Australians from other backgrounds.

Billies are used for boiling all foods, as well as for copious amounts of tea.
PHOTO: REG MORRISON

DODDER LAUREL
Cassytha melantha

The slender stems of this widespread parasite twine around their support in tight masses, often killing the host. When the stems have parasitically established themselves on the host by means of adhesive cushions, the plant becomes detached from the ground.

Dodder laurel produces small fruits crowned with the remains of the calyx. The flesh, surrounding a central stone, is very aromatic and tangy. A slightly reddish green variety found in the Hawkesbury area of New South Wales is quite delicious and refreshing. Another common name is 'devil's twine'.

Small fruit of the dodder laurel, a pervasive parasitic vine of southern and eastern Australia.

40 DODDER LAUREL

*Dodder laurel (*Cassytha melantha*) growing in the Hawkesbury area of New South Wales.* PHOTO: JENNIFER ISAACS

EMU BERRY
Grewia retusifolia

This small upright shrub grows in shaded grassy areas of open forests and has many uses for Aborigines. It bears small dark red or orange double fruit with a very small amount of reddish pulp surrounding the seeds. The taste is pleasant, a little like that of seedy tamarinds or figs. This fruit has been known to Europeans since the explorations of Ludwig Leichhardt, who reported gathering large quantities and making refreshing drinks by boiling the fruit. 'The beverage was the best we had tasted on our expedition', he wrote. The plant has medicinal uses as well.

On a recent bush tucker expedition the children, in particular, leapt from the vehicle to gather the berries and ate them immediately.

*Emu berries (*Grewia retusifolia*). These taste like very seedy tamarinds or figs.* PHOTO: JENNIFER ISAACS

EMUS

Emus are highly thought of as bush tucker because of the quantity of their meat and the delicacy of their flesh. Emu eggs are also sought and eaten, each mother bird laying several beautiful large deep green eggs. One of the most common techniques of hunting emus is to stun them by putting narcotic leaves in their waterholes. The poison most frequently used by northern desert people is *Duboisia hopwoodii*. As the stupefied bird walks slowly from the waterhole as if drunk, it is ambushed by the hunters from a brush fence. Other poisons are used in the desert including *Prostanthera striatiflora*.

Emus are usually cooked in a similar way to kangaroos, but after plucking and gutting, blood is often wiped over the skin. When cooking birds the ground oven may be lined with herbs or leaves and hot stones may be placed within the body cavity.

Preparing and cooking an emu in the traditional Pitjantjatjara style was a lengthy process. After killing the bird, the legs and head were tied together so that it could be carried effectively on the shoulder of the hunter. A pit was made as for a kangaroo and the body was prepared for cooking. To keep it clean it was laid on green leaves and branches. First it was plucked, then completely skinned through a narrow aperture cut along the legs and behind the anus. The skin was pulled off the body as though it were a jumper. This skin was then turned right side out and stuffed with grass and feathers. The opening of the skin was closed with two pointed sticks and it was rolled in the flames to stiffen and brown.

The body was prepared for cooking by cleaning out the intestines and filling the space with a wad of emu feathers or sticks. The head of the bird was pushed into the body cavity through a hole in the neck and the whole bird, together with its stuffed skin, was cooked in a ground oven for half an hour or so depending on its size. The feathers used as stuffing were, of course, removed and discarded before the meal began.

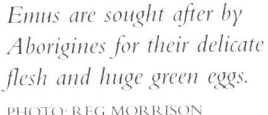

Emus are sought after by Aborigines for their delicate flesh and huge green eggs.
PHOTO: REG MORRISON

Overleaf: Emu family, Warrumbungles. PHOTO: REG MORRISON

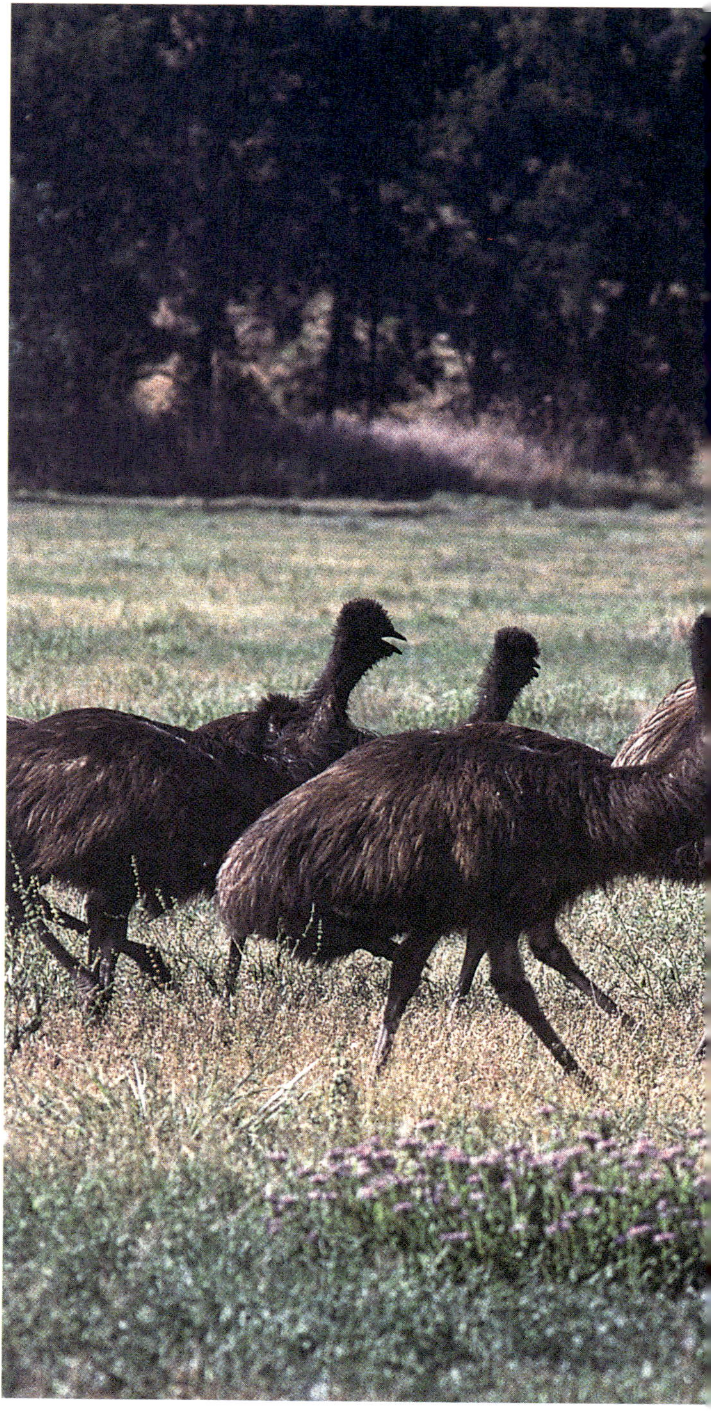

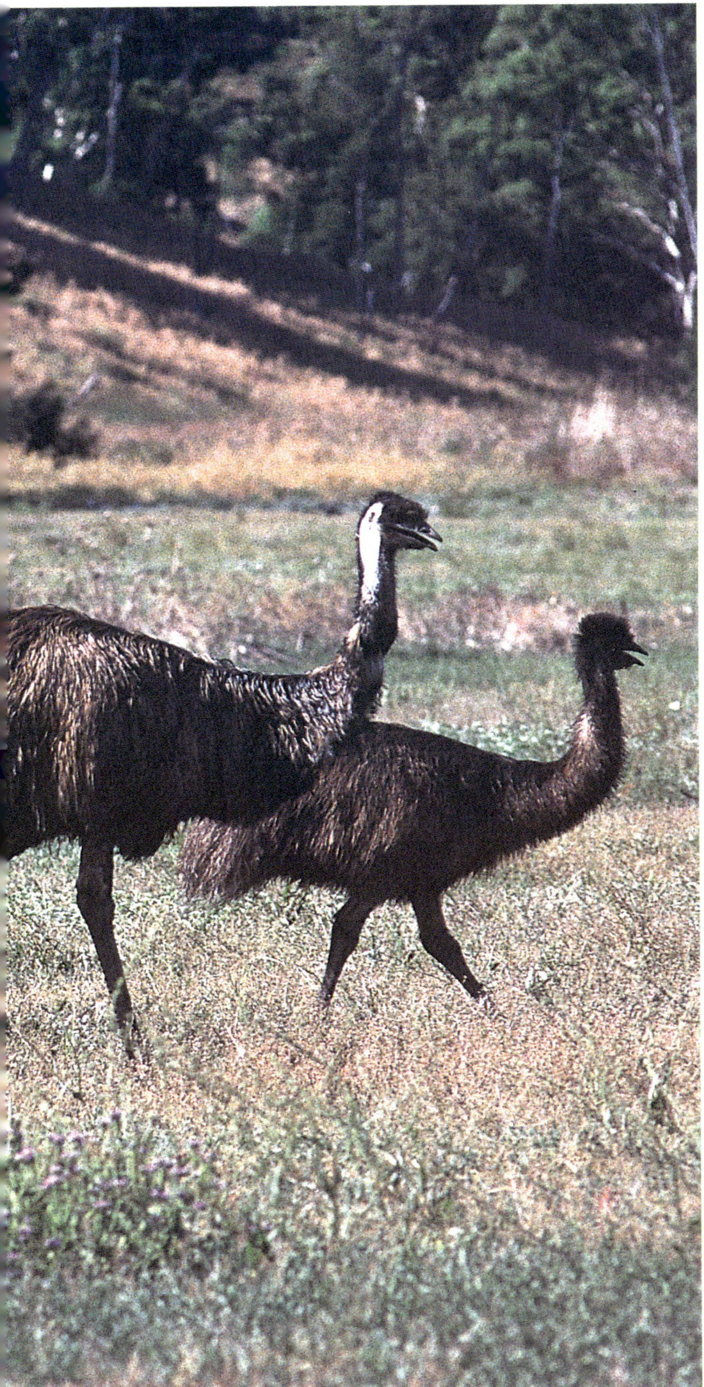

FERMENTED BEVERAGES

It is commonly believed that Aborigines had no alcoholic beverages among their traditional drinks. It is well known, of course, that the nectar of various flowers was gathered and soaked in water and then drunk, but reports of settlers also suggest that some techniques of using nectar and gum produced a state of euphoria.

At Bunbury in southwest Australia, a drink called *mangaitj* was made by soaking the flower heads or cones of grass trees (*Xanthorrhoea* spp.) in water in bark troughs. This mixture was allowed to ferment for several days and was reported to make people excited and voluble. Old accounts refer to the people of Roper River fermenting pandanus in order to make an intoxicating drink. *Pandanus spiralis* was prepared by beating the fruit between heavy stones and soaking the pulp in water for some time to 'extract as much of the palatable ingredient as possible'. The infusion was left up to several days so it could ferment. 'A refreshing toddy' similar to a mildly intoxicating cider was produced. On ceremonial occasions the drink was prepared some time earlier and the people had more than usual, which produced in them 'a condition of indubitable merriment'.

FIGS

Ficus spp.

Most Aboriginal people eat some kind of native fig. Although all figs are theoretically edible, several are more readily eaten because of their better taste and texture. Some figs appear as small pairs at the base of the leaf; others grow in clusters on stems and trunks. They vary from pea size to around 5 centimetres in diameter.

The Moreton Bay fig, well known on the east coast, has small fruits about 2 centimetres in diameter that are just palatable when dark purple. 'Sandpaper' figs, more common in the north, have much better flavour. The leaves of this species (*Ficus opposita*) are very rough, hence the common name, and were once used by Aborigines to smooth spear handles and boomerangs.

The desert fig (*Ficus platypoda*), or *wijirrki* in Warlpiri, is an appetising fruit loved by Aborigines in arid regions from Western Australia to New South Wales. It grows mostly in rocky outcrops in crevices where water and soil debris collect, or at the base of rocks where water run-off ensures

Cluster figs from a small patch of rainforest near Ramingining, Northern Territory.
PHOTO: LEO MEIER

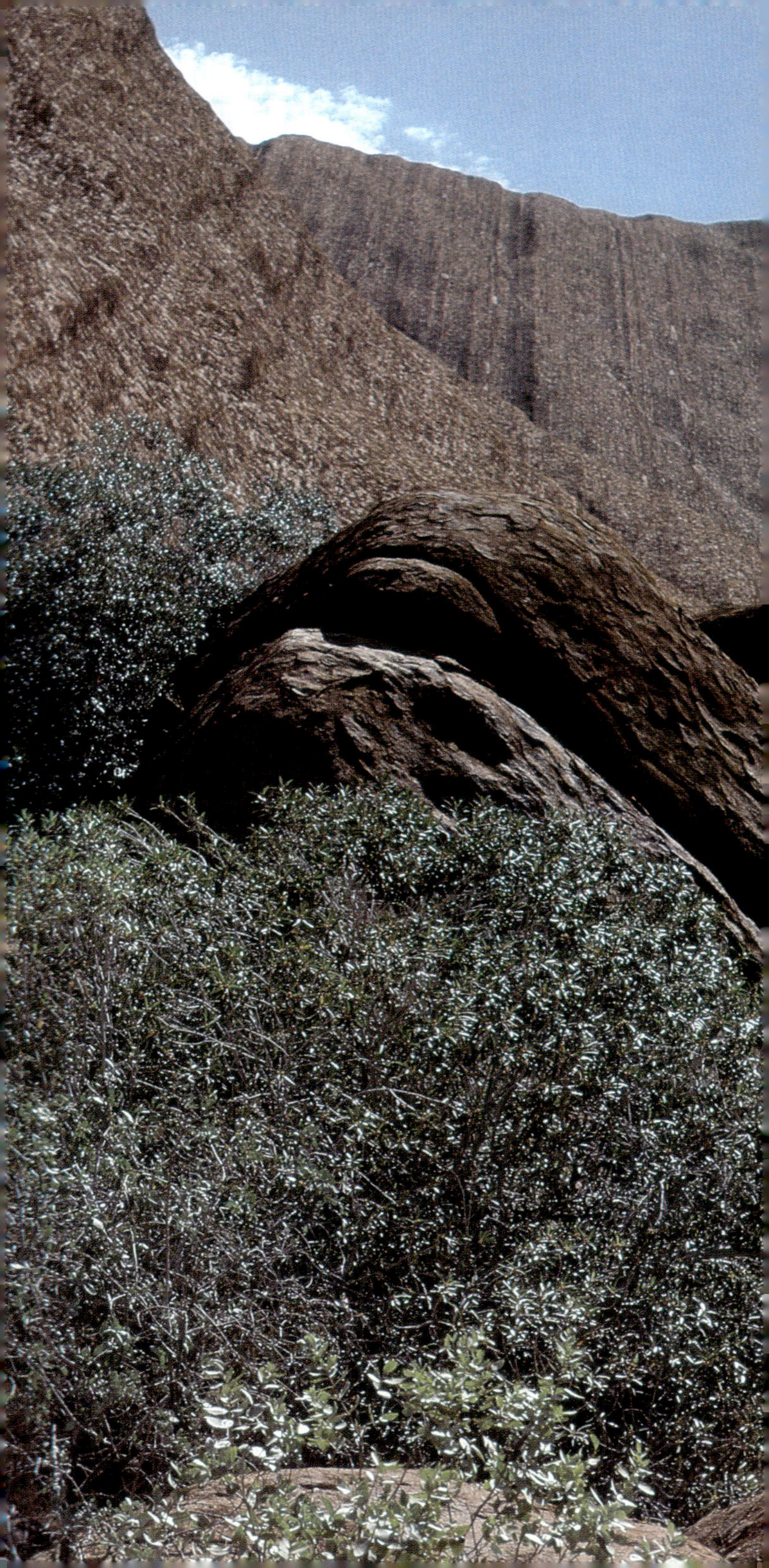

fertile soil. Individual trees may be quite large and bear thousands of fruits. The figs are yellow in their immature stage and turn red, orange or brown when ripe. They are usually eaten raw, straight from the bush. Food analysis shows that they have a good protein and fat content and some trace elements. The sandfig (*Ficus superba*) abounds in northeastern Arnhem Land. The fruits may be up to 2 centimetres in diameter and are eaten green, though they are sweeter when brown and fully ripe. The trees grow in sand close to beaches and fresh water.

Another Ficus variety commonly termed cluster figs (*Ficus racemosa* var. *glomerata*) is found in forests in north Queensland and the Northern Territory. The fruits grow in heavily laden bunches on branched stalks hanging vertically from the trunk. Although eaten by Aboriginal people wherever they occur, they are not as sweet and tasty as other varieties and are not prized as food. *Ficus racemosa* has a high water content, with traces of protein and fat.

FILE SNAKES

Several snakes are caught and eaten by Aboriginal people but the file snake is one of the most favoured. This large, harmless, wide-bellied reptile inhabits lagoons and swamps, and is generally caught in the water by women on turtle-hunting expeditions. Small file snakes can often be seen in

*Opposite: Wild fig trees (*Ficus platypoda*) are always found on rocky outcrops usually in association with a watercourse or waterhole. These bushes are growing near permanent water at the base of Uluru (Ayers Rock).* PHOTO: DIANA CONROY

billies in the camps, either kept as children's pets or waiting to be cooked on the fire. Their skin is very rough, like sandpaper.

When caught, the file snake is killed by holding the head in the mouth and giving the body a sharp yank downwards to break the backbone. The snakes are cooked whole on the coals.

File snake. These are found in northern Australian waterholes and are hunted for food.
PHOTO: LEO MEIER

FLYING FOXES

Flying foxes are eaten by Aborigines throughout the north. Large colonies can be found in deep jungle areas of the forests and in the mangroves. Flying foxes feed on the blossom and fruits of certain trees and, depending on the season, the flesh of the animal takes on the taste of these flowers and fruits and becomes aromatic and sweet.

Flying foxes are usually beaten from their roosts with long sticks; occasionally a fire will be lit beneath the tree and they will be smoked out, the smoke tending to stun the animals so that they drop to the ground. During the day, when they are sleepy and not alert, they can be knocked down with throwing sticks. The fur is first scorched off and the leathery wings are removed. The little bodies are then cooked quickly on the coals or in a ground oven. The flesh is soft and rather like chicken but very aromatic, with a flavour suggesting a fruit and honey diet.

In the north, flying foxes are a favourite meat in the flowering season, when their flesh is sweet and scented from the blossoms on which they feed. PHOTO: LEO MEIER

FISH COMMONLY EATEN

NORTHERN WATERS: QUEENSLAND,
NORTHERN TERRITORY, NORTHERN WESTERN AUSTRALIA

COMMON NAME	ALTERNATIVE NAMES	SCIENTIFIC NAME
Barramundi	Giant perch	*Lates calcarifer*
Barramundi (freshwater)	Dawson River salmon; Saratoga	*Scleropages leichhardtii*
Mullet	Many types, including Bully, Flat tail, Sand mullet (20 species)	*Mugil cephalus* (most common) *Liza vaigiensis* (Diamond-scaled mullet)
Catfish	Eel tail catfish	*Tandanus tandanus* (most common)
	Forktail catfish (8 species)	*Neoarius australis* (Blue catfish)
Shark	Many species	
Groper	6 species	*Cheilinus undulatus*
Barracuda	Sea pike	*Sphyraena barracuda*
Sawfish	Sawshark	*Pristis zijsron*
Snapper	Spangled emperor	*Lethrinus nebulosus*
Salmon	Threadfin salmon	*Eleutheronema tetradactylum*
Whitefish	Queenfish; Leathery	*Scomberoides Iysan*
Kingfish	Giant trevally	*Caranx ignobilis*
Bonefish		*Albula vulpes*
Sardine	Pilchard	*Sardinops neopilchardus*
Bream	Several species	*Acanthopagus berda* (most common)
Garfish	Many species	*Hemiramphus* spp.
Longtom	Garfish	*Ablennes hians*
Jewfish	Mulloway	*Argyrosomus hololopidotus*
Rock cod	More than 20 species	*Epinephelus* spp.
Coral trout	Coral cod	*Plectroploma maculatum*
Trevally	Many species	*Caranx* spp.
Mackerel	Several species	*Scomberomorus commersoni* (most common)

FISH 53

SOUTHERN WATERS: NEW SOUTH WALES, VICTORIA, TASMANIA, SOUTH AUSTRALIA, SOUTHWESTERN AUSTRALIA

COMMON NAME	ALTERNATIVE NAMES	SCIENTIFIC NAME
Dusky flathead	Lizard	*Platycephalus fuscus*
Bream	Silver bream; black bream	*Acanthopagrus australis; A. butcheri*
Snapper	Squire; red bream	*Chrysophrys auratus*
Blackfish	Luderick	*Girella tricuspidata*
Mullet	Several species	*Mugil cephalus*
Tailor	Chopper	*Pomatomus saltatrix*
Jewfish	Mulloway	*Argyrosomus hololopidotus*
Salmon	Australian salmon	*Arripis trutta*
Herring	Tommy ruff	*Arripis georgianus*
Trevally	Blurter	*Caranx* spp.
Murray cod (freshwater)		*Maccullochella peeli*
Golden perch	Yellow belly	*Macquaria ambigua*
Silver perch (freshwater)		*Bidyanus bidyanus*
Catfish (freshwater)		*Tandanus tandanus*

(Table courtesy Julian Pepperell)

Catfish cooking. Fish are gutted, then laid on their backs on the coals.
PHOTO: JENNIFER ISAACS

GEESE, DUCKS, IBIS AND WATER BIRDS

Although guns are generally used when hunting birds near billabongs or swamps, many ingenious traditional techniques were once employed. In the southeast of the continent large nets were strung close to billabongs and flocks of water birds were frightened so that they flew off and were trapped in the nets. Another rather humorous practice, also from the southeast, was for a hunter to swim undetected underwater until directly underneath the ducks on the surface. Then, with a sharp tug, he would pull the ducks beneath the water by their feet and render them helpless. Geese could be tricked by imitating the cries of other geese. As they came down from the high branches, they were quickly beaten with sticks or, in some areas, with boomerangs.

Yellow-billed spoonbills. PHOTO: REG MORRISON

GEESE, DUCKS, IBIS AND WATER BIRDS

Boomerangs, one of the most ingenious weapons used by Aboriginal hunters, came into their own in the hunting of birds. They were thrown into flocks as they were landing on water or taking off. The returning boomerang was thrown in a downward motion toward the ground. It then kicked up into the flock of birds, stunning or killing one so that it fell to the ground.

The goose egg season in Arnhem Land was described vividly by ethnographer Donald Thomson. The hunters and their families moved to the swamps where they built houses to await the coming of the geese and their nesting. Elegant flotillas of bark canoes headed out into the wide waters to catch geese and gather eggs, returning at night to special platforms built over the water, where the men feasted and slept.

Other birds caught near billabongs and swamps include pelicans, ibis and ducks. They are usually shot and carried back to camp for plucking and cooking. Large birds such as pelicans, ibis, and brolgas were once cooked in ground ovens. Today it is quite common to see fresh birds boiling in large billies.

Jabiru, Northern Territory. PHOTO: LEO MEIER

GOANNAS AND LIZARDS

Goannas and lizards are by far the most common traditional game of the desert regions.

Looking for goannas is hot work. Groups of women and children, occasionally accompanied by their husbands and fathers, head off into the desert to the areas where goannas may be plentiful. Occasionally one might be found in a hollow log, but usually it's a matter of finding an inhabited burrow. Avoiding unnecessary work is always the aim of the operation. These days, women carry digging sticks in the form of flattened crowbars. The entrances are carefully examined for recently dislodged sand or tracks and any holes with debris in them are completely ignored as these were abandoned long ago.

The reptiles can dig in any direction from the entrance and are extremely quick at making an

Western desert goanna. PHOTO: REG MORRISON

exit under the ground. To find the direction of the burrow from its entrance the women plunge the metal digging stick into the ground in an arc about a metre from the hole. As soon as the stick sinks into the ground as though into a hollow the digging begins. The entrance is widened and the animal is dug out along its burrow with a woman hunter finally reaching in and hauling the animal out by its tail. Women know when they are getting close to the burrowing animal when the sand in their hands becomes moist.

Goannas and all manner of lizards caught in the desert are cooked briefly in the coals of the fire. The meat is tender, rather more chewy than chicken and rather oily. Many other reptiles are caught and eaten throughout desert regions, including various snakes, skinks and geckos.

GRASS AND HERB SEED

Panicum spp.; *Brachiaria* spp.; *Eragrostis* spp.

In addition to seeds obtained from trees and bushes, Aborigines utilise many nutritious seeds from grasses, herbs and succulents, most of which are short-lived and favour disturbed ground or a consistent fire regime to encourage fruiting.

Grasses of the *Panicum*, *Brachiaria* and *Eragrostis genera* seem to predominate and are common throughout the centre, particularly along watercourses and in floodplains or mulga areas. Although most seeds are very small, each grass bush bears heavily.

Armgrass millet, *Brachiaria miliiformis*, bears seeds 2 millimetres in diameter with a slight lustre; woollybutt grass (*Eragrostis* sp.) or *wangunu*, a staple of the Pintubi, is somewhat smaller. Both are wet milled and poured into the ashes to make damper.

GRASS TREE

Xanthorrhoea australis

This distinctive Australian grass tree – or blackboy as it is sometimes called by white Australians – was once a multiple source of food to Aborigines, especially in Victoria and New South Wales. The flower nectar, basal leaves and shoots were eaten.

Grass trees grow mainly on sandy heathlands at the edge of forests such as the Grampians in Victoria and the Hawkesbury area in New South Wales. The crown of spiky narrow leaves may grow

*Grass trees (*Xanthorrhoea *sp.), South Australia. The flowery spikes were once made into a sweet drink and the soft basal parts of new leaves were eaten.* PHOTO: REG MORRISON

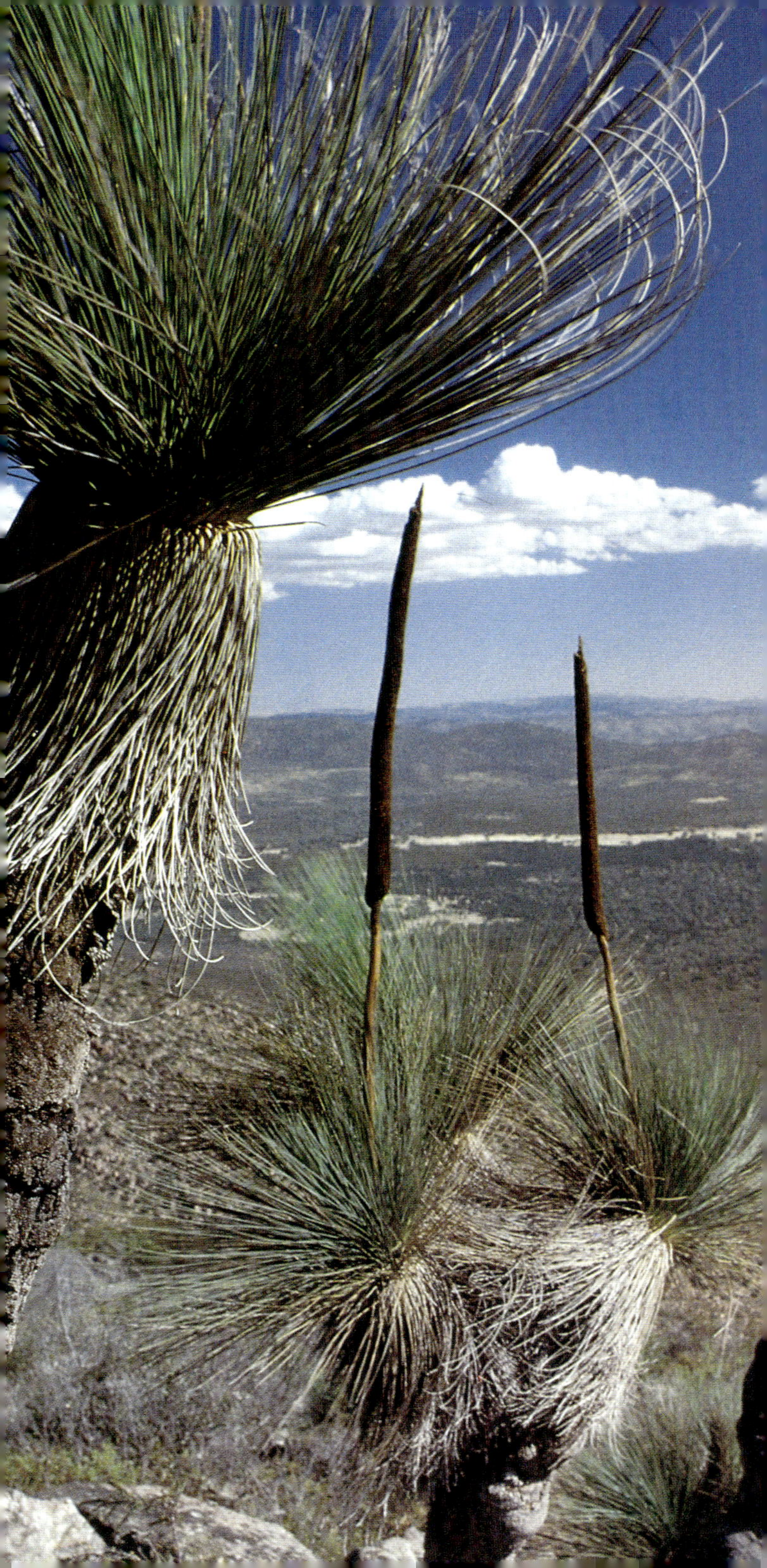

Grass trees in the Washpool rainforest, New South Wales. PHOTO: LEO MEIER

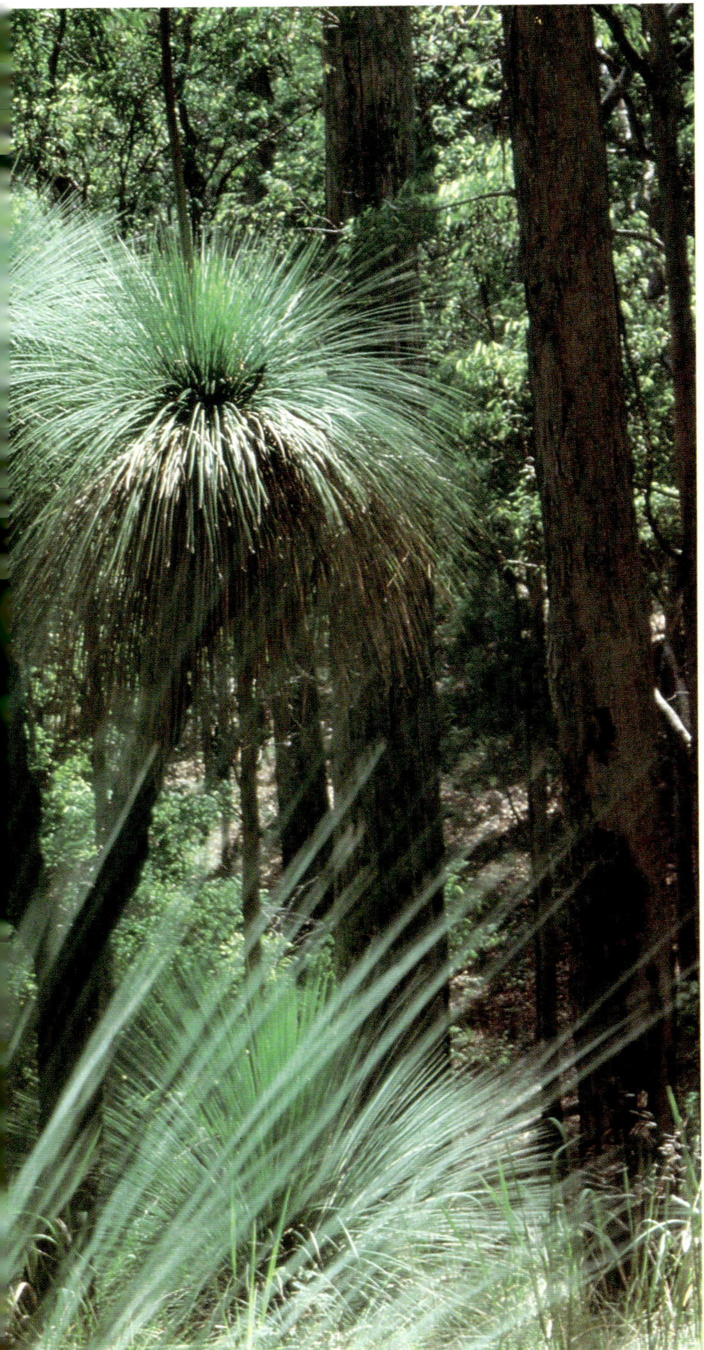

*A stand of grass trees (*Xanthorrhoea *species) survives bushfires in northwestern New South Wales.* PHOTO: MICHAEL COURTNEY

either directly from the ground or from a short or long trunk. The age of the plants can be determined by the height of the trunk. Early photographs of Aborigines show them scaling *Xanthorrhoea* 'trees' twice the height of a human. Today such specimens are extremely rare.

The flowering spikes of *Xanthorrhoea* were soaked in water to make a sweet drink and the soft basal part of the leaves was eaten. The growing tip of the stem could also be eaten, though this destroyed the plant altogether. The tall straight stems of the flower spikes, up to 150 centimetres long, made excellent light spear shafts. They were attached to the lower end of spears to extend their length and, therefore, range. The section of the spear closest to the tip was of harder wood that could withstand impact.

These beautiful plants are now protected species and cultivated examples are used as features in many landscape gardens.

GREEN ANTS

In the Kimberley region of northwest Australia during the growing time of the wet season, root crops become sour. To make them palatable people collect green ants' nests and squash the ants into pounded edible bulbs of the *Microstemma* species. This gives the food a lemony taste.

Green ants' nest.
PHOTO: JENNIFER ISSACS

GREEN PLUM

Terminalia ferdinandiana

The small fruit of these trees is common from northwestern Australia to eastern Arnhem Land, where it is termed *murunga*. Recently it has been drawn to attention as possibly the richest natural source of vitamin C in the world. Research carried out at the University of Sydney's Human Nutrition Unit, headed by Dr Jennie Brand, has confirmed that this fruit has more than fifty times more ascorbic acid (vitamin C) than citrus fruit. Terminalia are tall slender tropical trees with light green leaves and grow to 10 metres in height. The green fruits are about 2 centimetres long and 1 centimetre in diameter and contain one large pip. Brand commented that the fruit looks and tastes like an English gooseberry.

*The green plum (*Terminalia ferdinandiana*) is possibly the richest natural source of vitamin C in the world. These tart fruits are not staples but are regarded more as medicine or refreshments in the bush.*
PHOTO: VIC CHERIKOFF

The tart fruits are not a staple food for which Aborigines might go out on a special trip, but are devoured when in season by Aboriginal children. They are also eaten by adults on hunting trips for quick energy and refreshment and to quench thirst. The people of central Arnhem Land regard the fruit more as a medicine than a food, obviously with good reason.

GRUBS

It would seem that almost all grubs that look fat, white and edible, and that are found inside live trees and bushes, are edible, though they are palatable to differing degrees. In Tasmania long wood grubs, found in old timber and *Banksia* species, were eaten as delicacies, tasting to Europeans who tried them, 'like nuts or almonds'. In Victoria pupae found at the foot of gum trees were gathered and cooked in the ashes. These were apparently the pupae of processional caterpillars. Also in Victoria grubs were cut out of trees and eaten live 'with as much pleasure as a white man eats an oyster'. The hunters carried special small hooked wooden implements to insert into the trees and haul the grubs out. Another large, fat grub was found on the banks of marshes. These could be drowned out of their holes, cooked and eaten.

In Queensland, historical accounts speak of edible grubs found in 'dead' hickory trees, in bluegum saplings and at the base of the grass-tree *Xanthorrhoea* species. Hunters looked for borer dust on the ground beneath the trees and scaled them until they found the hole, or they noticed dead leaves in the centre of grass-trees and knew the larvae were doing their destructive work.

See also WITCHETTY GRUBS.

GUM

The resins that exude from ironwood, acacia and allocasuarina trees are a source of carbohydrate and may be eaten straight from the tree in balls like pliable toffee or melted with warm water to form a jelly. Although some are tasteless, casuarina gums are sweet and children enjoy these treats, leaping from vehicles when the globules are sighted on hunting trips in the north. Edible gums can be found all over Australia

In the southeast there are hundreds of species of wattle in many different habitats. As soon as summer was over, Aborigines cut notches in the bark to allow the gum to exude. It was often soaked in water with a sweet substance like honey, manna or flower nectar. The people of many traditional northern homelands maintain this technique of making drinks.

Often, after a hunting trip, when the meat is cooking and the wait seems long, young children look around for what desert people term 'bush lollies' and climb trees to pick off the gum to stave off their hunger.

H

HONEY see NECTAR, SUGARBAG HONEY

HONEY ANTS
Melophus bagoti

Honey ants are among nature's more extraordinary creations. As a means of drought endurance, the working ants gather honeydew and nectar from scale insects and psyllids and feed it to other workers who become mere nectar-storage vessels, or 'honey-pots', with tergum and sternum appearing as dark patches in the greatly distended abdomen. These helpless bloated ants are kept safe from the effects of drought in underground galleries and regurgitate some of their nectar to feed the other workers when solicited.

Women of central Australia, particularly in the desert areas of the MacDonnell Ranges, gather these ants from nests under mulga trees to rob them of the honey stored in their distended abdomens, swollen to the size of grapes. The nest consists of a vertical shaft, which may descend from 1.8 metres to 2.4 metres, along which horizontal shafts house honey ants in every chamber. The

Honey ant, a Dreaming ancestor and food source.
PHOTO: LEO MEIER

women must dig deeply to gather a small handful of prized ants.

Honey ants are particularly plentiful around Papunya, named for the ant itself – literally 'Honey Ant Dreaming' – and many contemporary Aboriginal paintings from Papunya are symbolic stories recounting the travels of the ancestral honey ant people to Papunya.

INSECT ACTIVITY ON PLANTS

The activities of insects on plants result in a number of edible substances including the galls on acacias, and lerp and crusty exudations on gum leaves. This sweet-tasting lerp or manna (to give it the biblical title) was once prized by Aborigines all over the continent, particularly in the southeast where it was enjoyed for its sugary taste and also made into drinks.

Bloodwood (*Eucalyptus terminalis*) galls are the result of the activities of an insect, *Apiomorpha pomiformis*, which feeds on the bloodwood's juices. The female insect burrows under the bark, irritating the tree so that it forms a gall around her. The grub or 'bug' has sucking but no biting mouthparts and lives inside the gall for its entire life.

Old galls can be seen on almost every large *Eucalyptus terminalis* tree in the MacDonnell Ranges. The juicy caterpillar and its watery surround are only found in fresh but 'mature' galls of light tan colour. The old dark brown ones are dry and inedible. On long hunting trips these galls offer people a small refreshing drink as there is sometimes a dessertspoon of liquid inside, as well as a juicy grub in its edible inner gall case. Among the Pitjantjatjara they are known as desert apples; in Alice Springs they are called wild coconut.

Smaller insect galls on mulga trees (*Acacia aneura*) are also eaten whole in desert areas.

Sugar bread. These sweet-tasting crusty patches on gum leaves are the results of insect activity.
PHOTO: HAROLD WELDON

Galls on bloodwood trees are formed by an insect. On hunting trips the galls are gathered and split to reveal a small, but refreshing amount of liquid and the edible grub.
PHOTO: LEO MEIER

INTRODUCED GAME: RABBITS, BUFFALO, PIGS

Since the mid-nineteenth century, when a handful of rabbits were released near Geelong, these animals have multiplied so dramatically that in many areas they have destroyed the fertility of the Australian landscape. In the desert south of Uluru (Ayers Rock), hundreds of rabbits block the roads at night and can be seen in the glare of headlights. Much of the land is potholed with rabbit warrens and they have largely replaced native marsupials of similar size such as the long-eared bilby. Bilbies were a significant source of food to Aboriginal people and rabbits have now usurped them in diet as well as landscape.

Rabbits are frequently eaten by Pitjantjatjara people. The women hunt them with digging sticks and they are dug out of their warrens in the same way as goannas. With a quick twist of the neck the animals are killed, the fur is scorched off and they are cooked on the coals.

In the north the water buffalo has become another threat to environment because of its habit of wallowing in billabongs and swamps, destroying the delicate balance of vegetation at the water's edge. Wild pigs pose a similar menace in Cape York and they are also widespread in Arnhem Land.

Although buffalo meat is welcomed in times of scarcity, it is not actively sought by Aboriginal people unless they are living on extremely remote outstations. Guns are needed and the animals are usually butchered, slabs of meat being cooked in the ground oven. Wild pigs are shot and cooked in a similar manner.

J

JUNGLE LAND SNAILS
Xanthomelon pachystylum

These snails, found under leaf litter at the base of trees in Cape York and Arnhem Land, are gathered, cooked and eaten. They are simply and quickly roasted on the coals and the snail flesh extracted as for nerites or periwinkles. In western Arnhem Land the shells are kept and decorated with dotted designs. They are tied in groups and clanked together to serve as musical instruments during ceremonies.

Jungle land snails are found in the leaf litter at the base of forest trees. They are occasionally eaten in Arnhem Land and Cape York after being lightly roasted at the side of the coals.
PHOTO: LEO MEIER

K

KANGAROOS, WALLABIES AND EUROS

When hunting kangaroos silence among Aboriginal hunters is usual, though sometimes whistles and signals communicate intentions from one man to another. People often work as a group, one man acting as a decoy while the startled animal stands motionless, staring. The others close in and freeze as the animal looks again. When speared or shot a wounded kangaroo is finished off immediately with blows to the neck. The animal is disembowelled the moment it is killed through a small incision made in the abdomen. The incision is then neatly skewered with a stick and bound in a figure-of-eight with the cleaned-out small intestine. The legs are dislocated and the carcass is either carried home on the hunter's head or, more frequently, taken to the waiting vehicle.

One interesting variation occurs in the Kimberleys, where at this stage the stomach, lower intestine and liver are removed, cleaned and boiled. The empty stomach is filled with fat and blood and

Dotted lines indicate the ritual division of kangaroo meat into portions.

rolled into a kind of black pudding. It is cooked in the earth oven with the kangaroo. The animal is tossed on to a blazing fire and turned several times until the fur has been singed and blackened. It is then removed from the fire and scraped so that the flesh is clean. The tail is usually cut off and placed beside the animal when cooking, though it can be left intact.

To prepare the oven a rectangular hole is dug about the size of the kangaroo to be cooked. A hot fire is made with plenty of wood in order to make a good supply of hot coals. The kangaroo is put on its back in the pit and the tail placed beside the body. The flesh is completely covered with hot coals, then with earth so that only the feet protrude. Cooking time varies depending on how hungry people are, and can be from three-quarters of an hour to four hours. If the hunters return late at night, the meat may be left in the pit overnight; in this case it is very well done.

When the animal is removed from the pit, the men gather to cut up the meat ritually. Women remain in the background waiting for pieces to be handed to them by their male relatives. This has been described as 'men's time'. In the desert the belly is opened and the rich blood soup is carefully drunk or poured into a billy and shared. The kidneys, heart and lungs are also shared. The meat must then be cut up by the hunter, each section going to an appropriate relative depending on his or her relationship with the hunter. It is quite common for the hunter to get very little himself. He must rely, in turn, on the success of a relative if he is to have one of the best sections of meat.

A male red kangaroo. PHOTO: LEO MEIER

This success depends not only on skill but also on the capacity of the hunters to deceive their quarry. Aborigines are brilliant mimics, both verbally and physically, and imitate the calls of birds, people's voices and movements. Emus are caught by preying on their inquisitive nature as hunters imitate other emus visiting from parts far off. Geese are brought down by hunters imitating their 'honk, honk, honk' in high branches and are then attacked with stones and sticks. Hermit crabs can be brought out of their shells with the high-pitched 'drrrrrr' sound of the tongue against the palate; the sound of a snake from a hunter's mouth will cause a bandicoot to leave a hollow log. Hand signals are an additional aid and the elaborate sign language recorded by people such as Walter Roth in northern Queensland at the turn of the century meant that, without speaking, hunters could communicate extremely well over large distances without alerting their quarry.

Hunting magic is frequently employed to ensure a successful hunt and the weapons themselves are often smeared with blood from a kangaroo. Many weapons are carved or painted in an act of ritual and faith. The decoration is not purely superficial but associates the weapons visibly with the ancestral spirits and gives them greater power and accuracy. Spear-throwers and spears may also be 'sung' to ensure that they do not fail.

Apart from simply spearing kangaroos, Aborigines use other, more ingenious, hunting techniques. Hides are constructed at waterholes and the animals speared when they come to drink.

Brush fences are constructed, behind which hunters can conceal themselves near a frequently used animal track. Other men, or more often women and children, beat the bushes to drive the game into the ambush.

This technique is sometimes used to catch euros, the lovely rusty red wallaroos that live on the rocks in the desert and leap about skillfully. Kangaroos are afraid of the rocky outcrops and will not mount them but the speed with which euros hop from one rock foothold to another makes it impossible for men or their dogs to run them down. The Pitjantjatjara hunt euros by utilising knowledge of their migratory pattern from one rocky outcrop to another. Euros fear the open plains and choose the shortest route between hills. Aborigines know these paths and conceal themselves behind trees along the track. Other men beat the animals to the concealed hunters or occasionally light bushfires that drive the euros ahead of the flames until they can be speared.

On the raised beach platforms of the Gulf of Carpentaria similar drives were once organised to catch wallabies. The beaches of the Gulf are covered with a modified jungle that forms relatively narrow belts of cover with open country on either side, kept so by regular burning off in the dry season. Wallabies could easily be seen feeding at night and early morning on the grasses of the plains, hiding in the jungle during the day. Hunting parties imitate the hunting call of the dingo and flush the wallabies out toward hunters hidden in specially constructed hides.

KONKLEBERRY
Carissa lanceolata

Konkleberries are large perennial shrubs that set fruit quickly after rain in desert areas. The small fruits last only a few weeks, though they may also be gathered dry. Known by various Aboriginal names, including *marnikiji*, they are a valuable food adjunct.

KURRAJONG
Brachychiton spp.

Red kurrajong	*Brachychiton paradoxum*
Desert kurrajong	*B. gregorii*
Black kurrajong	*B. populneum*

Tall, distinctive kurrajong trees grow all over the country and most of the seeds were once gathered and eaten by Aborigines.

In Arnhem Land, Cape York and Western Australia the red kurrajong bears distinctive single red flowers when the leaves have fallen, and the nuts that follow are still relished throughout the north. Although delicious, great care is needed. The nuts can be harvested either when the pods are green and mature or when they are brown. When green, the pods are collected in large quantities and baked in the ashes. When they are opened the whole of the pod contents, the seeds and their packing, are peeled out. The nuts pop easily out of the packing and can then be eaten. The packing, however, is very poisonous and must be thoroughly removed and the hands washed.

When the pods are a dull brown, the seeds inside are bright yellow. To prepare the nuts at this stage of maturity the packing and nuts are extracted and baked together. The fire tenders must sit with one side to the fire so that no smoke blows into their eyes. When baked, the sandpapery packing is rubbed off the seeds between the hands. The wind blows the poisonous 'hairs' away, leaving the clean

*The nuts of many species of kurrajong are delicious but require great care in processing. Seedpod and flowers of the red kurrajong of Arnhem Land (*Brachychiton paradoxum*).* PHOTO: LEO MEIER

The yellow kurrajong nuts must be treated carefully as the hairy packing in the pods is an irritant.

PHOTO: JENNIFER ISAACS

seeds, but again, the workers must sit so that the wind cannot blow the debris into their faces.

In central Australia the desert kurrajong, *Brachychiton gregorii*, replaces the red kurrajong of the north as a source of nuts. The people of the desert have an ingenius way of avoiding the toxic hairs and pith of the seed cases by gathering the nuts from the droppings of crows around waterholes – already cleaned of hairs and pith, but requiring cooking and dehusking. The nuts are baked in the ashes, removed from their 'skins' and pounded into a type of damper.

Another variety of kurrajong, *Brachychiton populneum* or black kurrajong, grows widely on rocky slopes in New South Wales and Victoria and is grown by farmers as drought fodder for stock. Southern people once gathered and ate these seeds which, when analysed by the University of Sydney team, were shown to have 25 per cent fat and 18 per cent protein, a most sustaining food.

L

LADY APPLE

Syzygium suborbiculare

Small lady apple trees, with their distinctive shiny red and green foliage, are prevalent along rivers and coastal cliffs of northern Australia, particularly Cape York. Along with black fruit they are eaten for variety in the diet, particularly by children, during the monsoon months from December to February.

LILLYPILLY

Acmena spp., *Syzygium* spp.

This large group of trees and shrubs has been known to Europeans since their earliest encounters with new flora, possibly even from the first visit of James Cook when Joseph Banks recorded a small

Lillypilly fruits (Syzygium spp.) may be pink, white or purple. The pink and white varieties were a popular Aboriginal food in the southern regions of Australia. PHOTO: VIC CHERIKOFF

red fruit. The clusters of berry-like lillypilly fruits may be cream with pink tints or deep pink to purple and are thick and pithy, sometimes slightly sour. They are eaten raw. The berries were also used for jellies by early settlers, and trees can be found in many suburban gardens.

In Victoria lillypilly occurs mostly in the gullies of East Gippsland, as far south as Wilson's Promontory. In New South Wales it is common on the edge of the rainforests of the north coast near Lismore. The trees can grow to 20 metres, though they are usually smaller.

LIZARDS, see GOANNAS AND LIZARDS

M

MANGROVE

Bruguiera gymnorrhiza

The hypocotyls of some mangrove trees are eaten, particularly in Cape York. During the wet season when people are confined to smaller areas and foods are hard to find, beaches offer a source of unusual food.

Bruguiera gymnorrhiza is a medium to tall tree that grows on intertidal sand and mud along tropical shores. It has rough, dark grey bark, knee-shaped pneumatophores and buttress roots. The distinctive flowers have rigid reddish green bell-shaped calyx lobes, which are found among tidal debris. The seed germinates while on the tree and the green hypocotyls or roots (looking like small

Mangroves, Hinchinbrook Island, Queensland.
PHOTO: LEO MEIER

Edible mangrove hypocotyls must be processed. These are Bruguiera gymnorrhiza, *known as* no'omb *at Weipa, and are often eaten combined with matchbox bean paste (*Entada phaseoloides*).*
PHOTO: JENNIFER ISAACS

thin okra) fall from the tree and are washed up. These are gathered and eaten after complicated preparation. The plant contains a high proportion of tannin and must therefore be leached. Quantities of *no'omb* are first baked in a *cup-mari* (Cape York ground oven) and the skins discarded. The food is then pounded into a pulp and soaked

Mangrove-lined salt waterhole, Western Australia.
PHOTO: REG MORRISON

in water. The mass is strained through a grass bag to remove excess water, then cooked again or mixed with cooked matchbox bean and eaten.

See also WHITE MANGROVE.

MANGROVE SNAIL

Telescopium telescopium; Terebralia palustris

This cone shell, which lies in or on the mud of mangroves, is one of the most interesting Aboriginal shellfish foods. When cooked, the flesh is bright green and, unless watching Aboriginal friends devour it with gusto, the colour would probably put most people off. Known as *congol* in Cape York, the shells abound in the mangrove areas around Cairns and can be collected at low tide. After being washed, they can be roasted in the coals, steamed over the fire on a wire grill or boiled in the billy. When the shells are roasted or steamed they are placed with the open end upward to retain

Congol, mangrove snails of the Telescopium *species, sit on the mud between the mangrove roots near Cairns, Queensland. After cooking, the turquoise flesh is extracted and 'stripped' before being eaten.*
PHOTO: JENNIFER ISAACS

liquid. The flesh literally boils in its own juice, and frothy bubbles can be seen coming out of the mouth of the shells.

Opening the shells is not easy. They are picked up from the fire when very hot and brittle and hit sharply in a circular motion around the perimeter of the mouth, each blow cracking off particles of shell and exposing more of the spiralling green flesh. Sometimes the shell is cracked in the centre and the two halves pulled gently apart so the flesh can be eased out.

In some parts of Arnhem Land and Bathurst Island these shellfish are eaten without cleaning, though those gathered in the mangroves near Cairns needed to be 'stripped' before eating.

MANGROVE WORMS, SHIPWORMS
Terodo spp.

Mangrove worms, or shipworms as they are known in other parts of the world, are the scourge of wooden-hulled boats, as they eat timber below the waterline. Although they look like worms,

'Shipworms' are actually bivalves which eat their way through the mangrove roots. They are relished as delicacies, eaten raw or cooked.

PHOTOS: REG MORRISON

these evil-looking delicacies are actually bivalve molluscs. Their shell plates have been modified to a tiny pair of abrasive plates at the head end. The worms are found in the intertidal roots of mangroves, often in the wood that has collected between the branched elbow-like supports that spring out from the trees into the mud.

There are two types of mangrove worm: a small white one and a long grey-pink one. The small white worms must be cooked; if eaten raw this type makes the throat sore. They are usually boiled in a large shell in the coals. The juice formed in the cooking is then drunk. The longer pink worms are eaten raw. They can be up to 30 centimetres long and 2.5 centimetres wide and have a 'lid' and 'teeth' which must be removed, along with the tail. The insides are usually sucked out or 'milked' and discarded, then the whole worm is eaten.

MARINE MAMMALS

Aborigines generally separate scale fish and small marine creatures from large 'meats' such as sea turtles, dugongs, dolphins and whales. The language itself clearly divides these classes of animals. There are distinctive words in Arnhem Land for animals with shells and for those with twin flukes on their tails or skin. Five different kinds of turtles are harvested in the northern waters: green turtle (*Chelonia mydas*), flatbacked turtle (*Chelonia depressa*), Pacific ridley (*Lepidochelys olivacea*), hawksbill turtle (*Eretmochelys imbricata*) and loggerhead turtle (*Caretta caretta*). The dugong, a beautiful sea mammal that gave rise to the legend of the mermaid, is also hunted and eaten by Aboriginal people. Whales were relished last century along the southeast coast. When they inadvertently beached themselves along the coast, the news would spread and hundreds would gather to feast.

MATCHBOX BEAN
Entada phaseoloides

Like the Moreton Bay chestnut the matchbox bean, or *dhapul* as it is called at Weipa, has to be processed to remove toxins. The seeds or nuts from

Rainforest at Dorrigo, New South Wales. Rainforests were once significant food sources for Aborigines, offering an array of fruits, nuts and small creatures. The growing tips or core of many species of palms were also delicacies. PHOTO: LEO MEIER

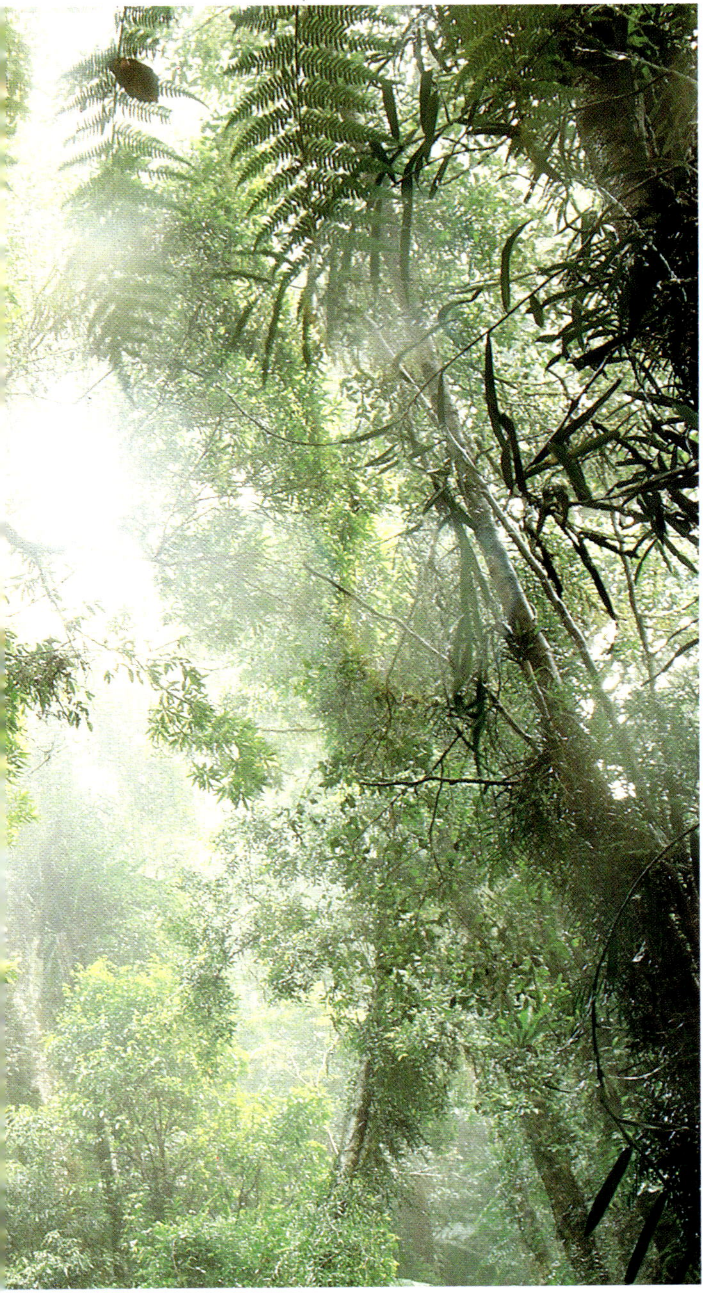

this open forest tree are available in all seasons. First the hard brown shells are cracked open and the white kernels removed. These are roasted, then grated or pulverised, after which they are soaked for several days before cooking again. When the nut meal is soaking in string bags it is frequently squeezed to remove the water.

Matchbox beans. PHOTO: JENNIFER ISAACS

MITCHELL GRASS

Astrelba pectinata

This seed-bearing grass was named after Major Thomas Mitchell, who explored western New South Wales and opened the way for pastoralists to settle in the area. Mitchell travelled along the Bogan, Darling, Lachlan and Murrumbidgee rivers and commented on the intense 'farming' of this grass by Aborigines. In 1835 he observed racks of the grass drying in the sun along the Darling River and noted that the grass grew saddle high as far as the eye could see. These were the stores of the Bagundji people, who had a remarkable seed-collecting economy. The seeds were gathered, ground and made into damper. Large quantities of stored seed were found long after the local people had been displaced.

When pastoral properties were established and the Bagundji stopped firing the grasslands, the grass crops soon failed. Scattered around most outback stations are the remains of this great seed economy – flat, well-worn grinding stones left at specific places until next season's visit because they were too heavy to carry. Many were left never to be used again.

MORINDA; CHEESE FRUIT
Morinda citrifolia

This small tree is known throughout Arnhem Land for the yellow dye that can be extracted from its roots and used by women for weaving pandanus.

The large, squashy fruit is an important medicine and is also edible. It fills the palm of the hand and can be broken into segments of swollen translucent flesh. It is greenish white, and has the strong smell and taste of Roquefort cheese. Local names for the fruit in eastern Arnhem Land include *burukpili* and *guninyi*.

Guninyi or cheese fruit (Morinda citrifolia).
PHOTO: REG MORISON

MORETON BAY CHESTNUT see BLACK BEAN

MUD CRABS
Scylla serrata

Like oysters, mud crabs are part of international cuisine. Although well known in the general Australian diet they are, nevertheless, expensive delicacies. To coastal Aborigines they are a delicious, easily obtained seafood staple.

Mud crabs, as the name suggests, inhabit burrows in the intertidal mud on the edge of mangrove areas and are particularly plentiful in settled tropical areas. A crab hunt is rather like a goanna hunt in the desert. When the burrow, or hide, is located the women plunge sticks into the mud in an area some distance from the hole until the crab is located and

Mud crabs are simply roasted in their shells on the coals of a fire until they turn orange.
PHOTO: REG MORRISON

dug out quickly. The crabs are always cooked immediately at the edge of the beach. They are placed on the fire until they turn orange and then removed. All the flesh and intestines are eaten, including the juices, fat and eggs.

MUD OYSTER

Batissa violacea; Polymesoda coaxans

These most prized bivalves lie hidden from view beneath the grey-black mangrove mud. They lurk beneath buried rotting mangrove branches and among the 'legs' of the mangroves, the branching elbow-shaped roots that reach into the mud to

A quick hot fire is lit over the shells which burns itself out in minutes. The shellfish are removed immediately they begin to open so that no delicious juices will be lost.

PHOTOS: JENNIFER ISAACS

support the mangrove colony in heavy tides. Sometimes the women find one shell on its own. Others are found in groups. The women walk slowly, heads down, bodies bent forward, feeling in the mud with their toes and the ball of the foot as they go, or tapping the mud with a long digging stick, machete or metal bar held vertically. If the implement makes a dull resonant 'clak' the shells have been found. If the mud is drier, or if a layer of sand has been deposited over the mud on the edge of the mangroves, slight cracks might be seen, sometimes with the end of the shell just visible, and the shells are quickly dug out. They can be almost as big as the palm of the hand.

Large bivalves are cooked in similar ways across the entire northern coastline of Australia, with small local variations. After being washed to remove mud or sand, the shells are placed in rows abutting each other, with 'heels' up and 'lips' down. In some areas the shells are placed directly on the sand. A quick and hot flaming fire is made over the top of the shells. The fire is important – too long and slow a heat will make the shellfish tough. The fire must get very hot immediately and burn itself out in three to five minutes. The charred twigs and ash that cover the shells are then flicked off with a fresh green branch of casuarina and the shells can be opened and eaten hot. Inside are large, succulent shellfish swimming in their own juices, aptly named 'mud oysters' and deserving of as much culinary acclaim as mud crabs.

MULGA

Acacia aneura

Although as many as twenty desert species of acacia have edible seeds, by far the most common and important food sources are mulga bush, *Acacia aneura*, and witchetty bush, *A. kempeana*, both of which form dense stands close to each other in the central desert region. Mulga bushes seed prolif-

*Distinctive grey-green mulga tree (*Acacia aneura*).*
PHOTO: DIANA CONROY

*Mulga seeds and pods (*Acacia aneura*).*
PHOTO: LEO MEIER

ically only when rainfall is reasonable and the mulga looks 'green', not its usual dull grey.

Mulga trees carry pods from 2.5 to 3.7 centimetres long, containing three seeds. The pods are collected from the tree, threshed and winnowed to separate them. Most accounts indicate that mulga seed is soaked or roasted before being ground and eaten.

Among the Pitjantjatjara and related peoples further south the mulga bush is known as *wanari*. Here the ripe seeds are ground into coarse flour, mixed into a paste and eaten raw. The trees are also useful for their many small waxy red growths (*wama*) found on the twigs. These are gathered, pounded up and infused in water, to be drunk as a sweetish tea. The process obviously varies from one group to another.

All acacia seeds analysed for their food content by the University of Sydney proved strikingly rich in nutrients with higher energy, protein and fat than crops such as wheat and rice, and even higher than some meats.

Mulga seeds and pods being winnowed over a coolamon.
PHOTO: LEO MEIER

NARDOO

Marsilea drummondii

Nardoo is a type of fern found in all states of Australia. It sometimes grows in the dry ground at the edge of lakes, though more usually it is aquatic with leaves like four-leaf clovers floating on the water's surface. The spores, produced in sporocarps about the size of a pea, were once gathered for food. Nardoo bread is mentioned in the journals of explorers Burke and Wills as being somewhat unpalatable, though it satisfied their hunger.

Nardoo is no longer gathered and eaten, but accounts describing its use indicate that Aborigines ground the spores between stones and removed the black husks. The remaining yellow powder was mixed with water for damper. Clearly it was a food for hard times, a hunger mollifier rather than a sustainer.

*Nardoo (*Marsilea drummondii*). The seeds make a damper eaten as a staple during drought.*
PHOTO: REG MORRISON

NATIVE GINGER

Hornstedtia scottiana

Native ginger is a much loved Aboriginal food, offering a pungent lift to the senses. This aromatic plant is found in swampy areas and small heartshaped fruiting bodies at ground level contain the seeds. The small seeds appear to be wrapped up in little packets, which are sucked. They are very sweet.

NATIVE RASPBERRY

Rubus parviflorus

The small red fruits of the native raspberry, common in wet sclerophyll forests of Victoria and New South Wales, are gathered and eaten raw. These are never a staple as the fruits are not plentiful, but their agreeable taste probably adds some interest, as well as useful vitamins, to forest travellers on hunting and gathering expeditions.

*Native raspberry (*Rubus *sp.)*
PHOTO: JENNIFER ISAACS

NECTAR

Nectar-bearing flowers are common in spring in bushlands throughout Australia from the coast to the desert. Aborigines gather bottlebrush, grevillea, banksia, hakea and the grass tree and suck them for

Grevillea *sp. Numerous nectar-bearing flowers from species of grevillea, hakea, xanthorrhoea and banksia were sucked or drained to make sweet drinks.*
PHOTO: JENNIFER ISAACS

Nectar-rich Grevillea eriostachya *at Uluru (Ayers Rock).*
PHOTO: JENNIFER ISAACS

their sweet taste. A type of liquor or drink is made in many parts of the country by immersing nectar-bearing flowers in water. When the diet is relatively monotonous, sweet nectar provides a pleasant lift to both taste and scent. In Queensland, when the dew is still on the grass and plants and the air perfumed and fresh, men and women gather nectar by going from flower to flower, dipping them up and down in a container of water until it becomes sweet.

Honey from the blossoms of the corkwood trees (*Hakea suberea*) is gathered by women of central and western Australia. The flowers are collected and kneaded in a coolamon. After the flowers have been removed, water mixed with the sweet residue makes a sweet drink.

In Victoria, *Banksia marginata* is a good source of nectar. It can be obtained by sucking the nectar directly from the spiky flowering cone or soaking the flower in water. *Banksia dentata* and *Grevillea pteridifolia* are similarly drained in Arnhem Land.

NEW ZEALAND SPINACH

Tetragonia tetragonoides

This green-leafed plant was once eaten by many of the southeastern Aboriginal communities, particularly along coastal areas. The stems and triangular leaves have greenish yellow flowers and crisp stems. The young shoots may be eaten as a green vegetable, cooked or raw. Joseph Banks took this plant back to England in 1772 where it became known as Botany Bay greens.

NONDA PLUM

Parinari nonda

Nonda plums of north Queensland are well appreciated, the Aboriginal name *nonda* being incorporated into the botanical name. The tree itself is large and has a weeping habit. The fruit is very important because it once sustained whole communities in September and October. The honey-brown coloured plums are usually gathered after they have fallen to the ground. When still firm the flesh leaves a bitter, unpalatable sensation on the tongue, like an unripe banana, but after a few days of sun-ripening the fruit are soft and mildly sweet, though surprisingly dry.

The nonda kernel gives highly nutritious milk when crushed and strained. This 'nut-milk' forms an admirable milk substitute in a culture where animals are not milked, but in which young infants are occasionally superseded on the breast by a new baby a little too early.

The nonda fruit are dried thoroughly until they resemble hard dry plums, then cracked between stones so that the white kernel is crushed. The pulverised fruit is compressed, squeezed and soaked in water in a bark trough. The milk that results is strained through fine grass baskets and given to babies and old people.

Nonda plums (Parinari nonda) of north Queensland. These widespread fruit once sustained whole communities. The plums are either eaten fresh after falling to the ground, or they are stored. When dry they are pounded and the mashed plums and kernels are soaked to make a thin white nut milk, popular as food for babies.
PHOTO JENNIFER ISAACS

Nonda plum kernals squeezed with water to make nut milk.
PHOTO: JENNIFER ISAACS

NUTS

Delicious nuts are found throughout the Australian continent. By far the largest number of nut-bearing trees occur in forests and rainforests, particularly in Queensland, where more than ten types of nuts are collected, processed and eaten by Aboriginal people.

See BAOBAB NUT, BUNYA PINE, BURRAWANG NUTS, BUSH CASHEW NUTS, CYCAD, KURRAJONG, MATCHBOX BEAN, PANDANUS, PEANUT TREE.

*Monkey nuts (*Hicksbeachia pinnatifolia*).*
PHOTO: VIC CHERIKOFF

OLD MAN SALTBUSH

Atriplex nummularia

A perennial shrub, the saltbush can grow to 3 metres in height and has bluish-grey leaves with brittle stems. The prolific seeds are ground into flour and made into damper in the drier inland areas, including Victoria and western New South Wales.

ORCHIDS

The small underground tubers of many species of terrestrial orchids are eaten in all Australian states, including species of the following genera: *Caladenia, Cryptostylis, Diuris, Dipodium, Geodorum, Glossodia, Lypernathus, Microtis, Prasophyllum, Pterostylis* and *Thelymitra*.

The Queensland tree orchid, *Cymbidium canaliculatum*, also provides food. The 'fruit' or pseudo-bulbs are eaten raw or grated and boiled. The thick starch gives this food the common nickname of native arrowroot.

Rock orchid.
PHOTO: VIC CHERIKOFF

Tree orchids of the Cymbidium *variety offer food in times of hardship as the false bulbs can be eaten raw or boiled.*

PHOTO: DIANA CONROY

OYSTERS

Hyotissa spp.

Oysters, part of international cuisine, are enjoyed by many people and are usually, though not exclusively, eaten raw. There are many Australian species. Aborigines prefer them all cooked, though most people eat at least half a dozen before bringing them back to the campfire. One favourite is the large black-lipped oyster, which can be found on the outer islands off the northern coast of Australia. Others include *Saccostrea tuberculata* and *Lopha folium*.

Oysters are collected in three ways. Sometimes they are tapped or hit with a heavy instrument such as a rock or a file so that the upper shell is cracked and the juicy flesh can be removed and put into tin mugs or bowls. Sometimes clumps of oysters are smashed off the rocks and carried back to camp in buckets. The third technique is used for varieties fastened on to mangrove roots. Then the root itself is cut off and carried back to camp, usually on the women's heads or cushioned in some way, as the shells are very sharp. Most women seem to sustain a few small cuts.

To cook oysters clumps of shells are turned frequently on the coals to expose all faces. The process is simple but delicate. It is important that when they are opened the oysters are still moist and juicy, and the cook is chided if they are 'dry'. When the clumps of oysters are cooked the flesh is removed by smashing the top with a rock or hard metal instrument.

See also MUD OYSTER.

P

*PALM see ALEXANDER PALM,
BURRAWANG NUTS, CYCAD*

PALM HEART
Livistona benthamii

There are two common *Livistona* palms in Arnhem Land: *Livistona humilis*, known as 'emu tucker' and called *dhalpi* in Yirrkala, and *L. benthamii*, called *gulwirri*. The latter is harvested for 'heart of the palm', one of the main vegetable foods eaten in bulk in north Australia. This harvesting kills the plant, though only palms of a certain height are harvested so whole stands are not wiped out. The palm may be eaten raw or cooked. It is crisp and clean with a delicious nutty flavour.

In the southeast of the continent the cabbage tree palm, *Livistona australis*, was once harvested and the unexpanded leaves of the tufted heads eaten raw.

PANDANUS
Pandanus spp.

The postcard sunsets of tropical Australia invariably use the silhouette of a pandanus tree as a symbol of the paradise of northern beaches. This distinctive branched, spiky-leaved 'palm' remains a very important plant of multiple uses to Aborigines. There are several pandanus species, often hard to identify by sight though *Pandanus spiralis* is the most important. The nuts or kernels from the large cones

Pandanus tree with ripe cone.
PHOTO: JENNIFER ISAACS

Pandanus seeds are embedded in the woody casing and must be prised out.
PHOTO: JENNIFER ISAACS

are eaten both raw and cooked. The fleshy basal part of the ripe fruit is also scraped or soaked and eaten. The soft white inner part of new leaves is eaten, as well as being stripped and woven into baskets that are essential for collecting and straining foods.

The heavy, hard, woody fruits, up to 20 centimetres in diameter, are made up of many individual segments, each of which contains seeds or 'nuts'. The seeds are removed from the plant only after the fruit has turned red and dropped in segments to the ground. This is extremely arduous work, requiring an axe or tomahawk to split the woody surround. It takes considerable physical effort to produce a small pile of nuts, and because of this many writers have wrongly assumed that pandanus are not important items of Aboriginal diet. In fact, pandanus kernels are eagerly eaten by Aborigines and the nuts are regarded as a luxury. During the fruiting season pandanus is a daily dietary component, though never a staple, and in order to collect enough nuts they are harvested and chopped almost every day.

In Cape York, if the fruit is slightly unripe it is roasted before being eaten. This cooking process helps to reduce the mild throat irritation that can occur from eating the basal part of the drupe. The pulp of the drupe is also soaked in water to produce a sweet drink. It is interesting to note that more than 140 years ago Ludwig Leichhardt observed a variety of pandanus debris in an Aboriginal camp. Following the example of the Aborigines Leichhardt scraped the soft end of the drupe with a knife and boiled the pulp. The resulting infusion was pleasant and 'did not affect the bowels'. Leichhardt mentioned in his diary that the natives seemed to live principally on the seeds of *Pandanus spiralis*. In their camp the pandanus was covered in hot ashes, roasted drupes were soaking in water-filled coolamons, and roasted soaked drupes had been put back on the coals.

When analysed at the University of Sydney, pandanus nuts were found to be very high in protein (between 24 and 34 per cent) and fat (44 to 49 per cent).

PEANUT TREE
Sterculia quadrifida

Known in eastern Arnhem Land as *balk-balk*, the bush peanut is one of the most delicious native nuts and requires no preparation before eating.

The nuts grow on small trees in thick, leathery pods about the size of a 20-cent coin. Each pod contains four or so large, shiny black nuts. The pods are initially green but turn bright orange or red when ripe, then darken to brown. The oval nuts may be gathered at any stage. The black skin of the nuts is removed with the fingernail and they are eaten raw by men, women and children out hunting. These nuts are regarded as 'pickings' rather than a staple food.

*Bush peanuts (*Sterculia quadrifida*) known as* balk-balk *at Yirrkala. These are delicious small nuts which do not require processing.*
PHOTO: JENNIFER ISAACS

PIGWEED
Portulaca oleracea; P. intraterranea

The prostrate portulaca herb is widespread from the coast to the inland desert, where it grows along sandy riverbanks. This succulent plant has opposed fleshy ovate leaves about 2 centimetres long. The stems sprawl along the ground. Small yellow flowers appear in summer, followed by capsules containing large numbers of minute kidney-shaped black seeds which, when piled in a heap, look like black sand. Each plant bears a large quantity of seeds and many can be collected quickly as whole plants are gathered and upended on sheets of bark or skin. The seeds fall out after some time and may be used fresh or stored for a considerable period.

Grass and herb seeds are stored for indefinite periods in desert areas, providing a predictable and safe supply of food in times of drought.

Although the seeds of portulaca are well known as a staple Aboriginal food made into damper, the leaves and stems also provide an important source of green vegetables. The plant grows widely in all states and has long been used in inland areas. It is a succulent plant containing a reasonable amount of mucilage. This food is rather acidic and bitter to the taste.

Portulaca, or pigweed, grows widely throughout Australia. Both seeds and leaves are edible.
PHOTO: VIC CHERIKOFF

Portulaca plants are found along dry desert riverbeds.
PHOTO: JENNIFER ISAACS

PIGS see INTRODUCED GAME

PIPIS

Marcia spp.

Pipis are well known in the shellfish diet of the Australian community and are regularly served in restaurants. They abound on Queensland beaches and are often used for bait.

Aborigines are expert at 'catching' pipis. The hunter must be a fast digger and have very sharp eyesight. As the tide turns and each wave laps the sand, pipis bury themselves deeper in the wet sand. They go vertically, leaving only a small hole or bubble visible on the surface of the sand. They are very fast and can descend 30 centimetres in a couple of seconds

Pipis, like most seafood, are only plentiful seasonally. These small bivalves are usually boiled in billies until they open a little, or they may be roasted gently on the ashes at the edge of the fire.

Shellfish are often cooked briefly on the coals at the side of the fire. When the liquid inside begins to froth they are quickly removed.
PHOTO: JENNIFER ISAACS

After being roasted at the edge of the fire shellfish are served on a bed of leaves.
PHOTO: JENNIFER ISAACS

PLUMS see BURDEKIN PLUM, DAVIDSON'S PLUM, GREEN PLUM, NONDA PLUM, WILD PLUM

POSSUMS BANDICOOTS AND ECHIDNAS

Small marsupials are usually cooked quickly. They are gutted and roasted directly on the coals. Care is taken to avoid overcooking so that the precious fat will not escape.

Bandicoots can be enticed from their hiding places or hollow logs by imitating the hiss of a snake and possums are hauled from trees with the aid of long hooked sticks. Echidnas are dug from the ground, their spines burned and pulled off and then cooked in the coals. These spines were once kept to use as awls for piercing possum skin rugs.

Q

QUANDONG

Santalum acuminatum

Quandongs stand alone among desert fruits because of their pleasant taste and texture and the size of their bright red fruit. The trees usually appear in open spinifex and mulga country as single specimens or in small stands. The large, globular fruit are so loved by desert people that it is uncommon to find a tree, whether in fruit or not, that does not have a 'ladder' against it – a broken branch of another tree leant against the trunk halfway up to aid climbers. Even domestic quandong grown in Alice Springs gardens are well known and frequented by Aboriginal visitors to the town.

The ripe red flesh of the quandong is dry but sweet and is eaten straight, though it is also dried and stored for future use. Small collections of the fruit are always brought back to camp to give to older people or to the family.

The distinctive textured seeds are strung and worn as body ornaments or necklaces and the fruit of some trees have a tasty kernel that is extracted when it can be heard knocking inside the stone. These oily kernels are either eaten raw or pounded so the oil can be removed and used as a cosmetic to smooth the skin of face and body, much as

Ripe red quandong fruits and seeds form a litter beneath the quandong tree in central Australia.
PHOTO: JENNIFER ISAACS

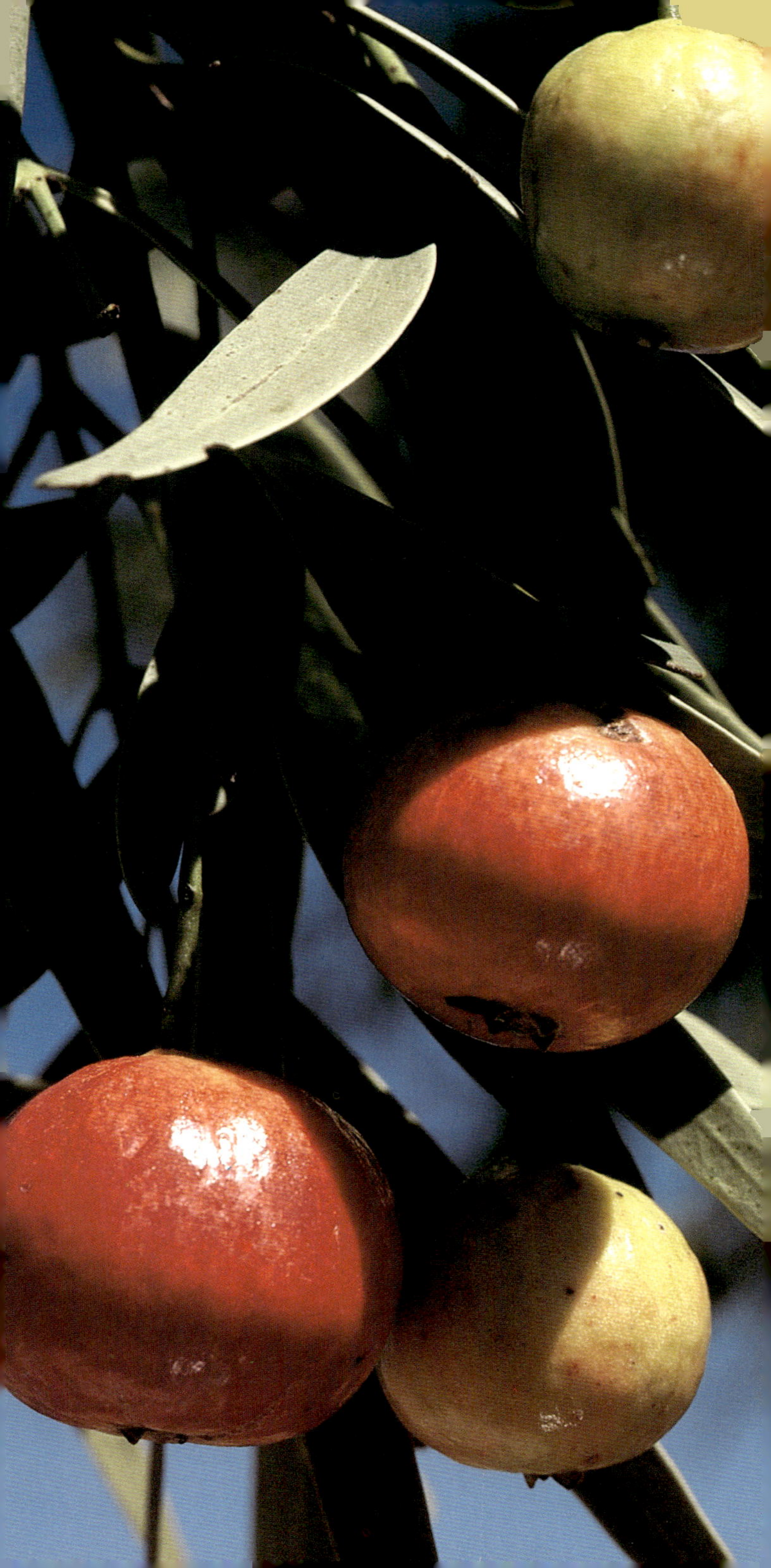

almond and apricot oils are used in European cosmetics. Aborigines know which trees have fruit with 'good' kernels and which might be toxic.

The fruit is rather acid and contains appreciable amounts of carbohydrate. It is high in protein compared with most fruit. Among some desert tribes it is considered such a valuable food that the CSIRO is currently investigating the possibility of commercial production.

R

RABBITS see INTRODUCED GAME

S

SACRED LOTUS

Nelumbo nucifera

The lotus differs from the waterlily in that its leaves are suspended on the stem above the surface of the water. The large pink flowers are followed by distinctive brown seed capsules.

The rhizomes of the lotus plant are used as food, particularly in western Arnhem Land. They have a high fibre content with good energy and carbohydrate levels and are sweet and palatable.

*Opposite: Quandong fruits (*Santalum acuminatum*).*
PHOTO: LOU MEIER

Spectacular blooms abound in the billabongs of the Kakadu National Park. These billabongs are inviting sanctuaries to Aboriginal families and offer abundant food.

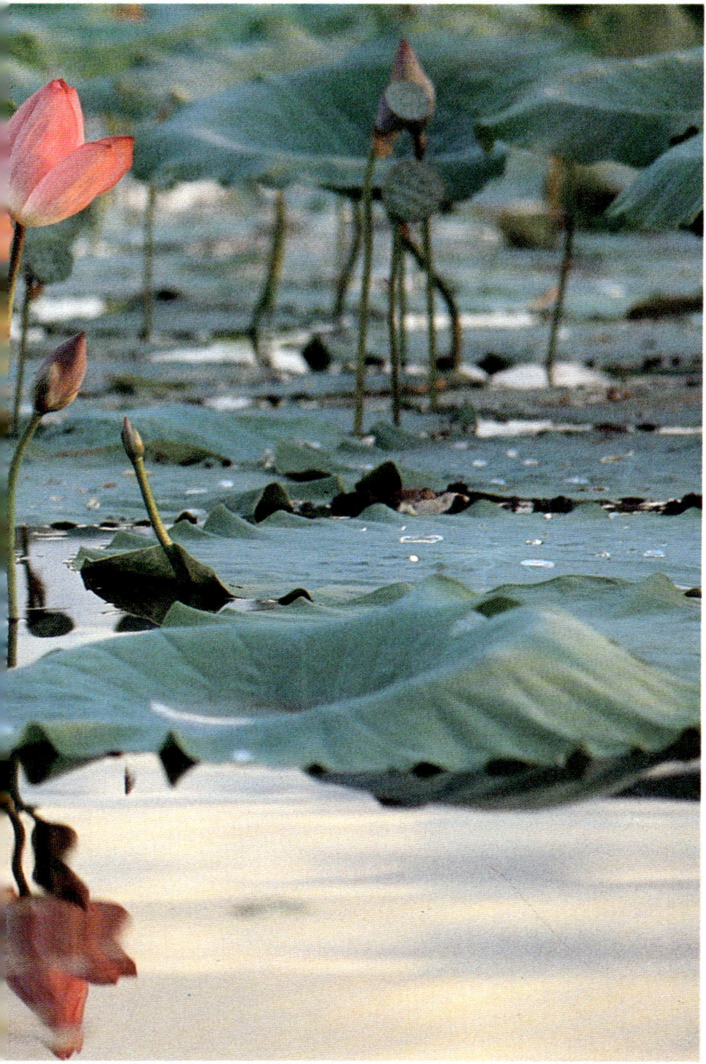

*Lotus flower (*Nelumbo nucifera*). These elegant plants of the billabongs of western Arnhem Land have edible rhizomes.*
PHOTO: LEO MEIER

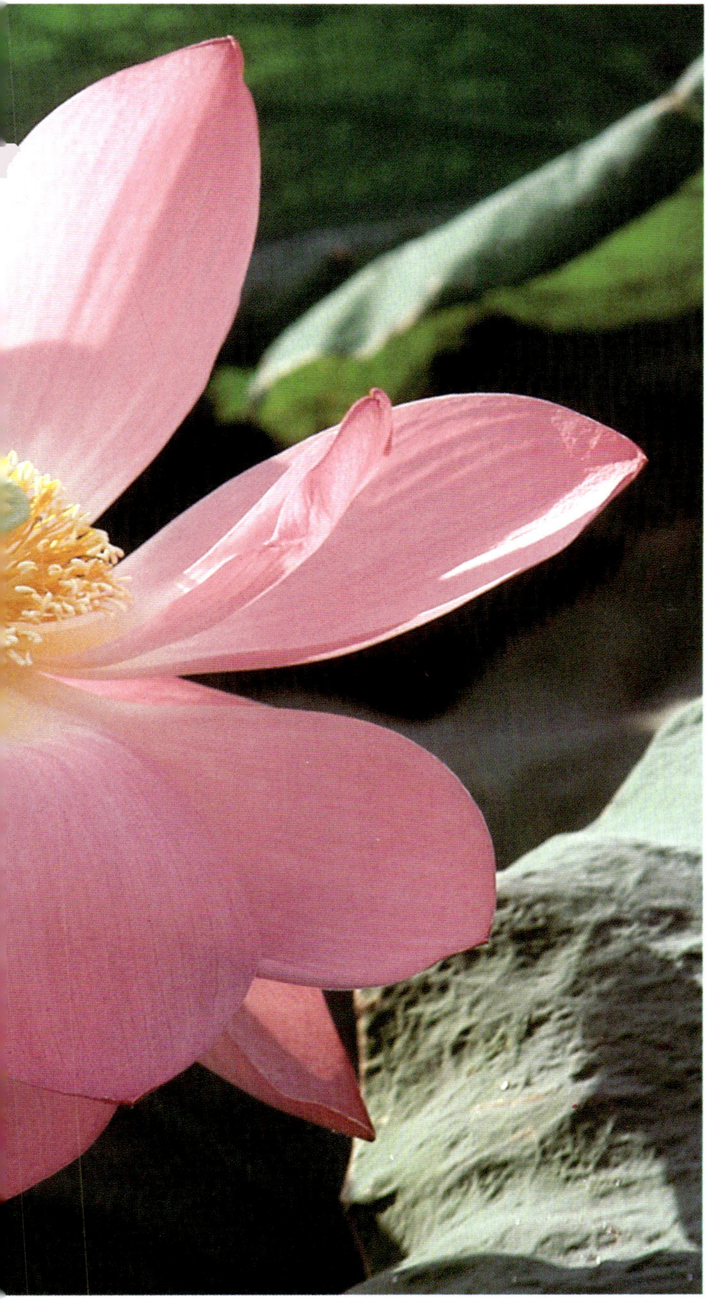

SHELLFISH

Some edible shellfish of the northern coast. Aboriginal names are those used at Weipa, north Queensland.

1. *'Congol'*, Conus figulinus
2. *'Acul'*, Batissa violacea
3. *'Drangol'*, Nerita lineata
4. *'Arrani'*, Melo amphora
5. *'Fundul'*, Trisidos yongei
6. *'Kumbuk'*, Anadara aliena
7. *'Kaanthuc'*, Hyotissa quirites
8. *'Evite'*, Lioconcha sulcatina
9. *'Armeg'*, Marcia liantina
10. *'Pipi'*, Donax cuneatus
11. *'Th'arr'*, Terebralia palustris
12. **Xanthomelon pachystylum**, *jungle snail.*

PHOTO: MICHAEL COURTNEY

SNAILS see JUNGLE LAND SNAILS, MANGROVE SNAILS

SPIKE RUSH; WATER CHESTNUT
Eleocharis dulcis

This thin rush grows profusely in swamps across the tropical north. The corms or chestnuts grow beneath the heavy dark soil of the swamps. The plant grows vigorously during the wet season and the first corms are dug out at the end of May or early June when the swamps are drying out. They are a delicious food still gathered in Arnhem Land where they are known as *rakay*. In Cape York they are called *ganj* and to the Lardil people of Mornington Island they are known as *panja*.

Good *panja* areas are traditionally 'owned' by the Lardil. To indicate ownership, clumps of the long rushes are tied into knots in a custom called *goohal*. The food provided by *panja* extends over long periods of the year.

Older, dark-coloured corms are roasted; younger, light corms can be eaten raw. After pulling them from the ground, the women collect the corms in bark containers, rinse them, bake them in the ashes for a few minutes and rake them out with a stick. The corms are then rubbed between the hands to remove the husks. Pounders and stones for grinding such foods were developed in Cape York where cakes of *ganj* were kept for up to two weeks.

SUGARBAG HONEY

Sweet nectar and honey is as much a delight in Aboriginal cuisine as a French cake is in the European. Although not a staple food, it nevertheless provides high energy and is eagerly sought, not only in northern Australia but throughout the continent. Even in arid lands grevillea, hakea and banksia flowers are drained of their nectar to make watery sweet drinks and 'honey ants' are uncovered from nests a metre deep to be drained of the honey stored in their abdomens.

There are six main native bees in Arnhem Land, two *dhuwa* bees and four *yirritja*, varying both in temperament and in the quality of their honey. Hives may be made in the top of eucalyptus trees, in mangroves and even in termite mounts. One particularly vicious *yirritja* bee, *niwuda*, sometimes attacks eyes. The honey of *niwuda* is slightly sweet but not as sweet as that from the *yarrpany*, the small, quiet bees. Two other *yirritja* bees have very sour honey: *milnhirri*, which build their hives in *manyarr* mangrove trees, and the yellow bees, *barnggiti*, which build hives close to the ground, sometimes in termite mounds. The *dhuwa* bees are *yarrpany*, a small gentle bee that nests high in trees, and *lirrawar*, a slightly larger bee whose hive is much smaller. Both *dhuwa* bees give very sweet honey.

Anthrolopogist Kim Akerman has identified three species of bees in the northern Kimberley area recognised by the Ngarinjin and Worora people: *namiri*, *narra* and *wanangka*. *Namiri*, which have thick treacle-like honey, build hives in the ground, under boulders, in antbeds and in hollow

Bush honey. All the contents of the hive are collected: honey, wax, yellow pollen balls and dead bees.
PHOTO: JENNIFER ISAACS

trees. *Wanangka* bees produce slightly runny honey, described by Aborigines as 'cool jam', and this is found in trees. *Narra* honey is very fluid, 'very cold and runny'.

In the Kimberley honey is a staple food, not just a luxury, and its importance is reflected in mythology, art and ritual life. In the past it was an important item in trade and beeswax had essential uses such as joining the seal on a bark bucket and helping attach a stone axe to its handle.

See also HONEY ANTS, NECTAR.

T

TOMATOES see BUSH TOMATOES, RAISINS, SULTANAS

TREE FERN

Dicksonia antarctica

Tree ferns and many similar ferns are found in gullies and rainforests throughout Australia. The soft pithy tissue near the top of the trunk contains a lot of starch and can be eaten either raw or cooked. Removing the pith, however, destroys the plant. Another tree fern once eaten is the *Cyathea* genus with eleven species common in moist gullies in southeastern Australia. The trunk was split open and the starchy pith eaten raw or roasted. In many areas, the 'fiddleheads' or unopened fronds were eaten. They had to be roasted to remove shikimic acid.

Tree ferns in the Grampians, Victoria.
PHOTO: REG MORRISON

TURTLES

Along the coast the turtles arrive with the southeast monsoons and swim to sandy beaches to lay their eggs. As they mate, canoeists head out to sea and wait patiently until they can see them. A harpoon is hurled at the animals and the men jump over the side of the boat or canoe and quickly turn the turtles on their backs. When the turtle has been immobilised on its back several men carry it up over the sand. Turtles are described

Turtle eggs in white sand at Yelangbara.
PHOTO: JENNIFER ISAACS

Leaves known as djilka *in northeast Arnhem Land are used in the ground oven to flavour turtle meat.*
PHOTO: JENNIFER ISAACS

as 'three man' turtle, 'four man' turtle and so on, depending on their size.

Large turtles are cooked in a unique way. The throat is cut under the neck near the hard breastplate and the intestines, liver and fat are pulled out of the hole. A large fire is built, rather like the kind set for an earth oven with stones or lumps of antbed on top. The turtle is upended in the sand and the hot stones or pieces of antbed are stuffed into the intestinal cavity. The neck hole is fastened off by a stuffing of special turtle leaves called *djilka* at Yirrkala. The meat inside the turtle shell roasts slowly for two hours, during which time the intestines and liver are cleaned and cooked, as well as the eggs if there are any. These are roasted on the coals and eaten as 'entrees' while the rest of the animal cooks. The plastron (lower shell) is levered off and the turtle's back acts as a bowl for holding the meat and juices while they are divided. The legs are cut off at this stage and thrown back on the coals to roast.

Turtle eggs are a delicacy prized for their flavour, nutrition and thirst-quenching qualities. They are soft shelled. When cooked, the yolk hardens but the white stays runny. Aborigines frequently 'drink' raw turtle eggs to quench their thirst while they are hunting for eggs.

The meat of long-necked turtles (*Chelodina* spp.) is a delicacy throughout northern Australia. Most freshwater turtles are snake-necked turtles, which hide their head or neck under the front part of the carapace, retracting them in an S-shaped curve.

When the waterholes are low at the close of the dry season women tread around the edge in the soft wet mud, raising their toes one after another in a pushing, dancing motion. If they reach a patch of mud that they cannot push down with their foot, they are sure there is a hibernating turtle below. Of all the hunted creatures turtles are the most easily caught, offering little resistance. In the wet season, when the waterholes are high, women must swim beneath the water to look for turtles among the reeds or watch quietly until the still waters reveal their small round heads bobbing to the surface for air.

Because the billabongs are often some distance from camp, turtles are usually cooked while the

Long-necked turtles hibernate in the mud.
PHOTO: LEO MEIER

women are out on the hunt, though some are always taken back home. A fire is lit and the turtle placed on the open flame. It is usually killed beforehand with a quick twist of the neck, but large and obstinate animals are put on the fire while still moving. After about ten minutes on its back on the open fire, the carcass is taken off. A slit is made under the neck and the intestine removed. The large intestine is cleaned out and thrown on top of the coals. It cooks quickly into a crisp, delicious meal, somewhat like roast chicken skin. The turtle itself is placed back in the coals. After cooking for twenty minutes on one side it is turned over and cooked on the other side for an equal length of time. To serve the meat the turtle is turned on its back and a slit is made around the plastron at the point where it joins the back, or carapace. The plastron is removed in one action, leaving the meat in one whole piece in the carapace, which acts as a bowl. It can easily be cut loose from the shell and divided into portions. The juices remaining in the carapace are drunk and it then used as a dish in which to divide the meat for members of the family

Turtle meat is extremely oily but delicious, and the entire animal is eaten except for the head. Cooked turtles can be transported and stored for a day or so.

W

WATERLILY
Nymphaea sp.

Throughout Arnhem Land there are three types of waterlilies in swamps and billabongs. The underground corms are gathered and roasted in the ashes. The blue waterlily is termed *wak wak* at Yirrkala, the pink is *dhatum* and the white is *burpa*. The women wade into the billabongs or swamps and dig with their fingers and feet in the mud under the plants to get the corms.

The processed corms are high in carbohydrate and fibre, and contain a significant amount of protein as well as water, fat and trace elements.

Waterlilies grow throughout Australia on swamps and billabongs. The way in which Aborigines, children especially, harvest them has been photographed frequently, epitomising for many the romantic view of a people at one with a tranquil landscape and enjoying the fruits of the billabong. Waterlilies may be white, pink or blue in Arnhem Land. The stems of all three are eaten as well as the fresh seeds from the flower bud and

WATERLILY

Waterlily seeds, stems and corms of the Nymphaea *species are all edible.*
PHOTO: JENNIFER ISAACS

Waterlily corms are collected by women from the mud, then washed in hand-woven pandanus sieves. Cooked for a short time in the coals, they are then peeled and eaten as a delicious meal. They can also be ground into cakes for children or the elderly.
PHOTO: LEO MEIER

Waterlilies in a paperbark swamp in eastern Arnhem Land.
PHOTO: JENNIFER ISAACS

*Seedpods of the northern Australian waterlily (*Nymphaea species*)*. PHOTO: JENNIFER ISAACS

the corm. Seeds are eaten direct from the capsule, though the raw stems must be peeled before eating. Stems are often carried back to camp in dillybags or chewed along the route as they are full of water and good for quenching thirst. The black seeds taste somewhat like poppy seeds and the stems take on the taste of the billabong itself, with a distinctive stringybark swamp smell of mulch and vegetation.

Waterlilies are not only foods; they are considered to be the morning star itself. In eastern Arnhem Land the spirits of the dead follow the light of Barnambirr, the morning star, on their way to the island of Baralku. The waterlily is the symbol of this star; its stalk is the path of the star across the sky, its flower the bright glow.

See also SACRED LOTUS.

WATTLE
Acacia spp.

Many species of wattle have edible seeds. These are generally collected when they are fully ripe, in brittle pods hanging from the branches. The pods are beaten heartily with a stick to release some of the seeds, and both the pods and remaining seeds are winnowed in a curved wooden dish or coolamon. The seeds of the Victoria wattle *Acacia victoriae* are roasted, then ground, and used in the food industry as 'wattle seed' flavouring.

See also MULGA, WIRY WATTLE, WITCHETTY BUSH.

WHITE MANGROVE
Avicennia marina

On Mornington Island in the Gulf of Carpentaria, fruit pods from the canoe-making tree are buried in hot ashes for around an hour. They are then peeled and soaked in water overnight before being eaten.

This food was once probably eaten by most coastal people with mangrove areas within their tribal lands.

WILD ARROWROOT
Tacca leontopetaloides

The explorer Ludwig Leichhardt may have given this species its colloquial name of arrowroot when he wrote in his journal:

I tried several methods to render the potatoes, which we had found in the camps of the natives, eatable, but neither roasting nor boiling destroyed their sickening bitterness; at last I pounded and washed them, and procured the starch, which was entirely tasteless, but thickened rapidly in hot water like arrowroot, and was very agreeable to eat, wanting only the addition of sugar to make it delicious — at least, so we fancied.

Although this tuber grows throughout the Top End of the Northern Territory, it is harvested and processed with elaborate skill only in Cape York. The tuber itself is not eaten but its starch is extracted, set and cooked in cakes. The processing of this food is perhaps the closest Aboriginal equivalent to the techniques of the horticulturists of Papua New Guinea.

The plants can be found in semi-shade relatively close to water. At Weipa they occur along sandy ridges around a kilometre from beaches. The plant has a double tuber, one old and dried, the other white and fresh. Only the new tuber is removed; the other is replaced to grow again. This harvesting takes place after the wet season, when the green growing time has passed. Indeed the tubers can be collected right through the Dry when a bare brown stem is the only visible evidence of the plant.

WILD DESERT ORANGE

Capparis mitchellii

This small desert fruit, which grows on a large shrub, is much admired by desert people but is found only infrequently in summer. It offers moderate energy, water and carbohydrate compared with other fruits, but is a good source of Vitamin C and thiamine.

Wild desert orange bush, Capparis *sp.* PHOTO: JEANNIE DEVITT

WILD GRAPES

Ampelocissus acetosa; A. gardinera

The wild grape is found throughout the north of Australia. It is common in Arnhem Land, the Gulf of Carpentaria and Mornington Island, where it bears fruit during the early part of the wet season.

Wild grapes
(Ampelocissus acetosa).
PHOTO:VIC CHERIKOFF

The vine grows in open forest, jungle or near beaches and appears annually from perennial roots. Clusters of grape-like fruits can be eaten when ripe; when the vine itself has withered and dried the roots are dug up and roasted. Among the Lardil the roots are called *dabum-dabum*.

WILD PEACH
Terminalia carpentariae

This large tree is found throughout northern forests. The green ripe fruit look somewhat like withered peaches before they ripen; the taste resembles a very dry peach. The local term for this fruit at Ramingining is *mardunggudj*.

WILD PLUM

The green fruits of *Buchanania obovata*, called *munydjudj* at Yirrkala, are only 1-2 centimetres in diameter and are eaten raw after discarding the seeds. This is an important north Australian fruit, which ripens in clusters from November to January. It is occasionally stored like dried prunes and when required, reconstituted with water.

Another wild plum, *Santalum lanceolatum*, is

*Wild peaches (*Terminalia carpentariae*). They taste like a drier version of their namesake.* PHOTO: LEO MEIER

smaller than the quandong and, though it passes through a red stage, is dark purple when fully ripe.

This is the fruit of the sandalwood tree, found widely over Australia and used in some areas for 'smoke medicine' because of its aroma. In desert regions the trees seldom reach more than a metre or so, though in mulga scrub close to creeks they can grow to 2 metres. In the desert the trees do not have the characteristic sandalwood scent. Among the Warlpiri they are known as *mukaki*. The fruits have been found to have a good water content, some protein and fat.

WILD RED APPLE

Syzygium sp.

This large red 'apple' is abundant from the end of the dry season. It has a very large stone and is a favoured food in Arnhem Land.

Red apple of Arnhem Land, Syzygium *sp.*
PHOTO: DIANNE MOON

WILD RICE

Oryza sativa

After the wet season wild rice grows extensively on the swampy plains around the Gulf of Capentaria. Aborigines process the grain by soaking it, then removing the chaff by rubbing the seeds in bark troughs. Alternatively, the grain is often burnt and the seeds removed from the ash, ground, mixed with water and baked. The grains are very like smaller brown rice.

WIRY WATTLE

Acacia coriacea

This hardy plant is known as *irkilli* to the Pintubi and *pankuna* to the Warlpiri of the western desert. *Acacia coriacea*, bearing the *irkilli* beans, grows to 3–4 metres high with a heavy crop of pods as long as 30 centimetres, each containing twelve or so large green seeds with an orange cap. The seed pods are gathered green and can be opened and eaten raw like green peas or cooked in the ashes. They have a delicious flavour like sweet beans. As the green beans appear during the dry season between September and November, they are a highly rated moist vegetable in Warlpiri and Pintubi country.

If the *irkilli* are to be cooked, they are lightly roasted in the fire and eaten. The cooked vegetable tastes rather like a chestnut, though it remains crisp.

In spinifex areas these seeds are a staple food as they are highly nutritious. The green beans have a high water and protein content, some fat, carbohydrate and fibre and good trace elements. When black and dry they offer very high energy levels, high protein, very high carbohydrate and fibre, some fat and water and good trace elements.

Delicious green beans from wiry wattle are known as irkilli *(*Acacia coriacea*) to the Pintubi.*
PHOTO: LEO MEIER

The wiry wattle has a distinctive formation and regenerates after fire. It offers a bounty of green beans or seeds.
PHOTO: HAROLD WELDON

WITCHETTY GRUBS

Cossidae spp.

Witchetty grubs are the most important insect food of the desert and a much valued staple in the diet of women and children. Men also love witchetties but seldom dig them. By the time the women have returned to camp, there are small pickings left, the women and children having already eaten well of the grubs in their raw state.

Witchetty grubs are found in the superficial roots of *Acacia kempeana* bushes, commonly known as 'witchetty bush' around Alice Springs and central Australia. A group of women, usually with older children, will always stop for witchetties if they come to a likely stand of bushes. These days flattened crowbars are highly regarded as tools as they require less physical effort than the older sharpened mulga digging sticks. Low to the ground, bending beneath the spreading branches, the women jab through the ground into the roots with the point of the bar or stick. It takes skill and practice to determine the direction of the roots by close examination of the hardened earth surface. The women move around the bush jabbing at roots until they feel them give. This indicates that they have located the grubs. Sections of root are then levered out of the ground or chopped off with tomahawks. The huge fat grubs may be 10 centimetres long and 2 centimetres in diameter, though many are much smaller.

The grubs are cooked quickly in the ashes, care being take to push away all coals. With a long stick

Witchetty grubs are eaten raw or lightly cooked in the ashes.
PHOTO: HAROLD WELDON

they are very gently rolled in the hot ash several times and checked from time to time. They swell and the skins stiffen. I have eaten these delicacies on many occasions and consider them a luxury food of world class unique to Australia. The skin is crisp, like roast chicken and the insides become solid and bright yellow like fried egg. They have frequently been likened to almonds in taste.

WITCHETTY BUSH
Acacia kempeana

Witchetty bushes are smaller and more spreading than mulga trees and are commonly found on spinifex plains. Their name stems from the

*Edible seeds of the witchetty bush (*Acacia *species).*
PHOTO: LEO MEIER

Opposite: A small group of edible pigface plants cling to the cliffs of the Great Australian Bight on the edge of the Nullabor Plain. Many foods of coastal environments throughout Australia were harvested seasonally by Aborigines. PHOTO: REG MORRISON

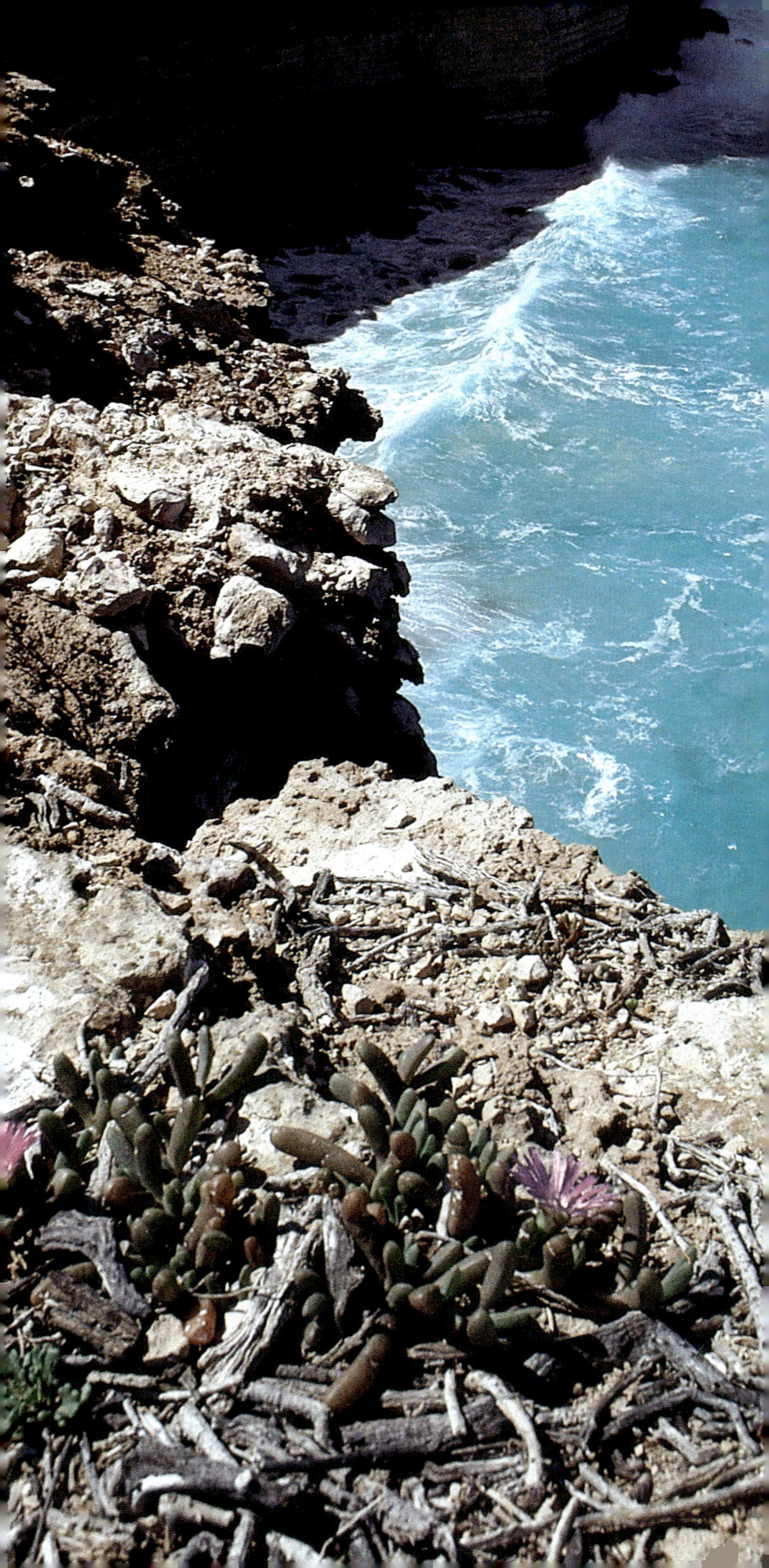

presence of the favourite desert food in their roots.

Seeds of *Acacia kempeana* are treated in the same way as mulga seed. Among the Pitjantjatjara they are known as *wintalka*. They are ground into a paste, mixed with water and eaten raw.

*Ripe brown witchetty bush seeds (*Acacia kempeana*).*
PHOTO: LEO MEIER

Y

YABBIES

Cherax spp.

In mainland estuaries or freshwater streams, yabbies or crayfish were a favourite Aboriginal food. Large species grow to 25 centimetres and are still hunted enthusiastically by country children. Pollution, over-clearing of agricultural land and introduced predators, such as carp and trout, have reduced their numbers but they are now commercially farmed and are offered on restaurant menus as a gourmet delicacy.

Opposite: Freshwater yabbie, Lamington National Park, Queensland. These delicacies were once widely hunted and eaten by Aborigines throughout Australia. PHOTO: LEO MEIER

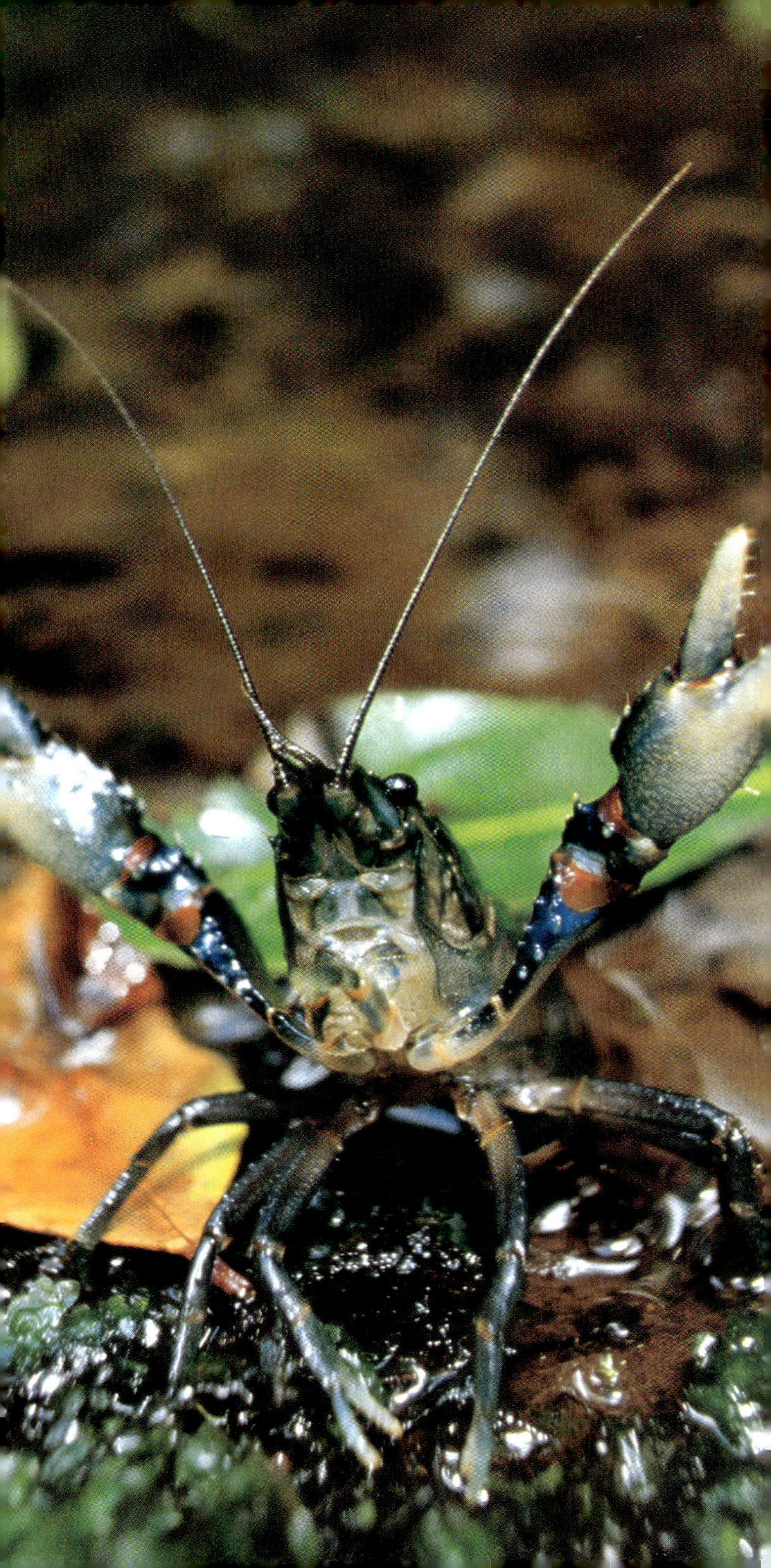

YAM

Dioscorea spp.

The desert yam *Ipomoea costata* or *yala* is one of the staple foods of central Australia. The yam, sometimes difficult to locate, grows up to 90 centimetres underground and is distinguished by runners, or dormant stems, when growing. The tubers can be very large when close to creeks and water supplies. The rounded tubers are 12–20 centimetres long and 5–18 centimetres wide and a single plant may have up to twenty yams.

The tubers are cooked under the coals. The hot coals are brushed aside and the yams placed on the warm earth before being covered with ashes for twenty minutes or so, depending on the size of the vegetable. When cooked the yams are peeled, though even the discards can be eaten and are chewed by the

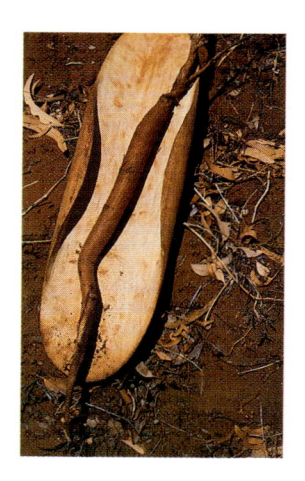

Long yams of the desert region, known as yala, are staple foods. Taproots like this, of some sapling trees, are also eaten.
PHOTO: LEO MEIER

In dense forests the presence of long yams is detected by vines bearing heart-shaped leaves, or, in the dry season, by the brown-winged seed capsules. PHOTO: JENNIFER ISAACS

Long yams, known as ganguri, *are washed and placed on a paperbark plate before cooking in a small ground oven. They have a slightly sweet potato-like flavour.*

PHOTO: JENNIFER ISAACS

children. This outer skin is tasty, rather like very stringy sweet potatoes but not as sweet.

These yams have a considerable percentage of moisture, with some protein and a little fat.

Long yam, *Dioscorea transversa*, is a species of yam commonly known in eastern Arnhem Land as *ganguri*, which once formed the most important source of carbohydrate throughout Arnhem Land and Cape York. The yams of this twining vine grow up to a metre underground and may be as slim as a pencil or multi-pronged and as long as a person's forearm. Small yams can be eaten raw, though they are usually cooked. In the early dry season the long yam can be recognised by its net-veined, heart-shaped dark green leaves; in the latter part of the year, when the leaves have turned yellow or dropped, it is recognisable by the seeds that hang in groups of dry, brown winged capsules.

Digging yams is still women's work. Groups of related women head into the bush with string bags and digging implements – crowbars flattened at one end, machetes or long, strong digging knives. In Arnhem Land the traditional wooden digging stick is now seldom used, though women will often quickly cut and sharpen a suitable implement from the stem or trunk of a young tree if a good food patch is found. The first places checked for yams are the most easily dug; loose-soiled sandy areas relatively close to camp. In northeast Arnhem Land women know from experience where the yams will be. Areas of open forest close to roads have long been harvested and people return to the same patches when they think the yams will be sizeable again.

With acute and trained vision the women follow the vines until they disappear in the grass, then feel for the point at which they enter the ground. Pushing the tall grass out of the way, they dig a narrow hole with their sticks, machetes or knives, beginning 60 or so centimetres away and at an angle to the presumed position of the tuber. But they can be wrong and some tubers are so far underground that it is not worth going on. When the yams are removed from the ground the women leave the vine stem and a small section of tuber in position and often push the earth back in the hole so the yams will form again.

The *ganguri* are washed and dried before cooking and some of the hairs on the skin are gently rubbed off. To cook yams the women build a small ground oven 30 centimetres deep and the diameter of a suitable saucepan for the quantity of yams they have found. They line the hole with coals, on to which the yams are placed and covered with ashes, coals and warm earth. The yams are lifted out after twenty minutes, put on a platter of leaves and given to everyone to peel and eat. These yams are quite firm and delicious and have a flavour rather like a slightly sweet potato.

YAM 145

*The round yam (*Dioscorea bulbifera*) of Arnhem Land and Cape York has many fibrous roots and requires cooking and leaching before being eaten. It has a slightly hot taste.*
PHOTO: VIC CHERIKOFF

The round yam (*Dioscorea bulbifera*) grows either in jungles or in very sandy soil. This yam, known as *jitama* in eastern Arnhem Land, is somewhat round and fat and is covered with numbers of fibrous roots. It requires more preparation than the simply baked long yam.

The round yam is either boiled or roasted in the ashes, then peeled, grated, pounded and soaked in running water for at least a day. The 'cakes' that result are 'hot' food.

Foliage of Dioscorea bulbifera. PHOTO: JENNIFER ISAACS.

YAM DAISY
Mieroseris scapigera

The yam daisy is a native perennial, similar to a dandelion and between 10 and 30 centimetres in height. The fleshy roots were once eaten by Victorian Aborigines as a staple food. The plant was dug widely along the rivers, especially the Yarra, Murray and Maribyrnong, where it had the common name of *murrnong* among Aboriginal people. The white tubers were either washed, scraped and eaten raw, or washed and roasted in fibre baskets. It is rather sweet with some seasonal bitterness.

Although no longer commonly seen in settled areas, the yam daisy is still found in the bush in some areas of southern Australia.

YELLOW LILY YAM
Amorphophallus glabra

This vegetable, called 'yam' by local Aboriginal people, is really the corm of a yellow lily found on the edge of dark patches of jungle in Arnhem Land. It can be dug during the dry season as the upright dried lily stems make it easily recognisable. The corm is large, round and squat, about the size of a fist, but its taste is not really admired.

The bulb, called *kanawarangi* or *lowiya* in the Djinang language, must be cooked in a ground oven or on the coals for a whole night.

The first scientific expedition to Arnhem Land in 1948 deseribed the cooking of *Amorphophallus* as follows:

The normal procedure [at Melville Bay and Port Bradshaw] was to make an oven early in the morning. A large layer of hot stones was covered with large green leaves, then the roots were put on top, then another layer of stones, more green leaves and finally paperbark and sand to close the oven. The oven was not opened until the following morning . . . Until it has been sufficiently cooked this corm has a very sharp flavour and leaves an unpleasant burning feeling in the mouth.

Paper bark swamp, northeast Arnhem Land. Paperbark is used to close earth ovens. PHOTO: JENNIFER ISAACS
Overleaf: Cycads in Kings Canyon, Northern Territory.

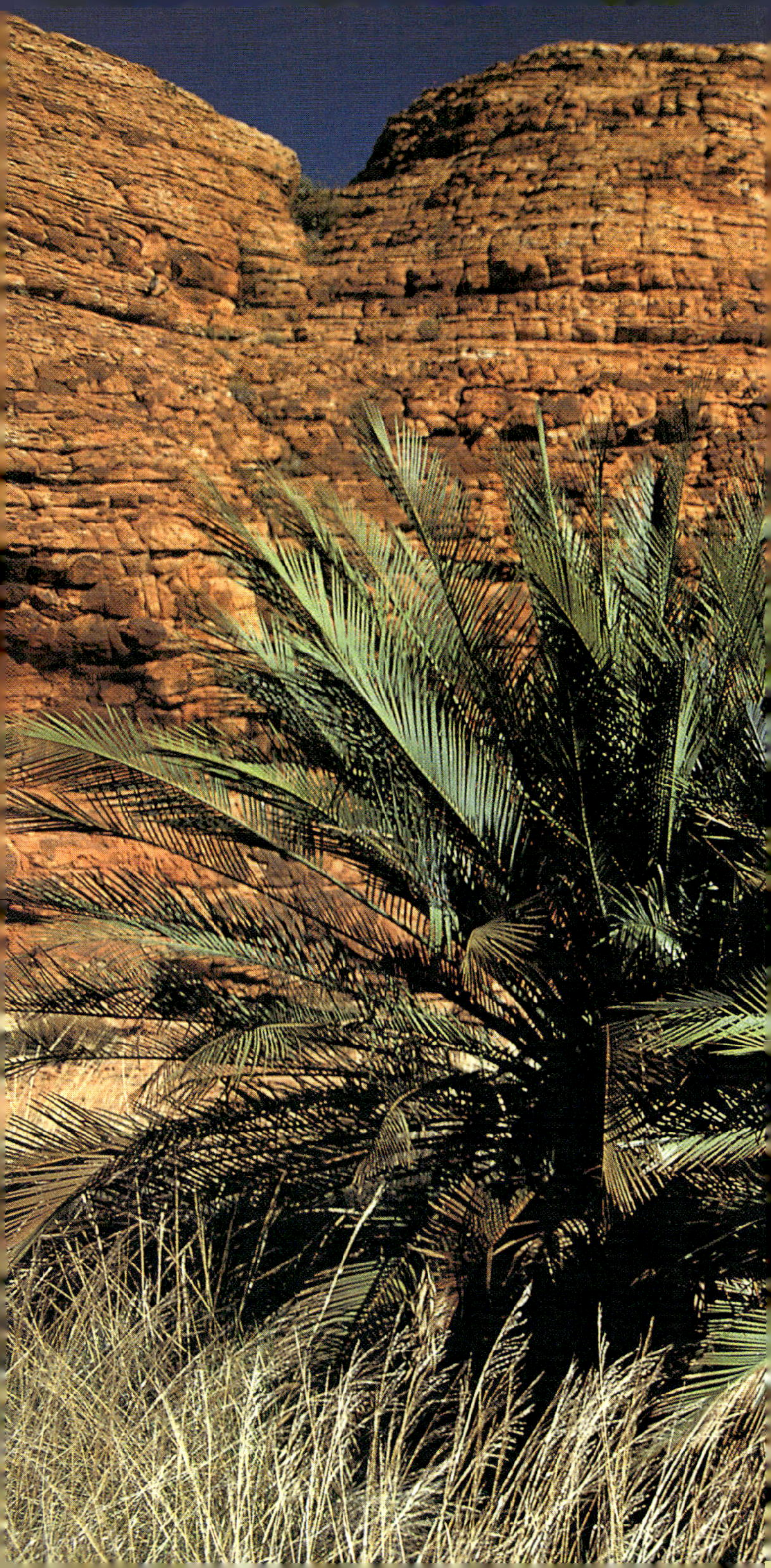

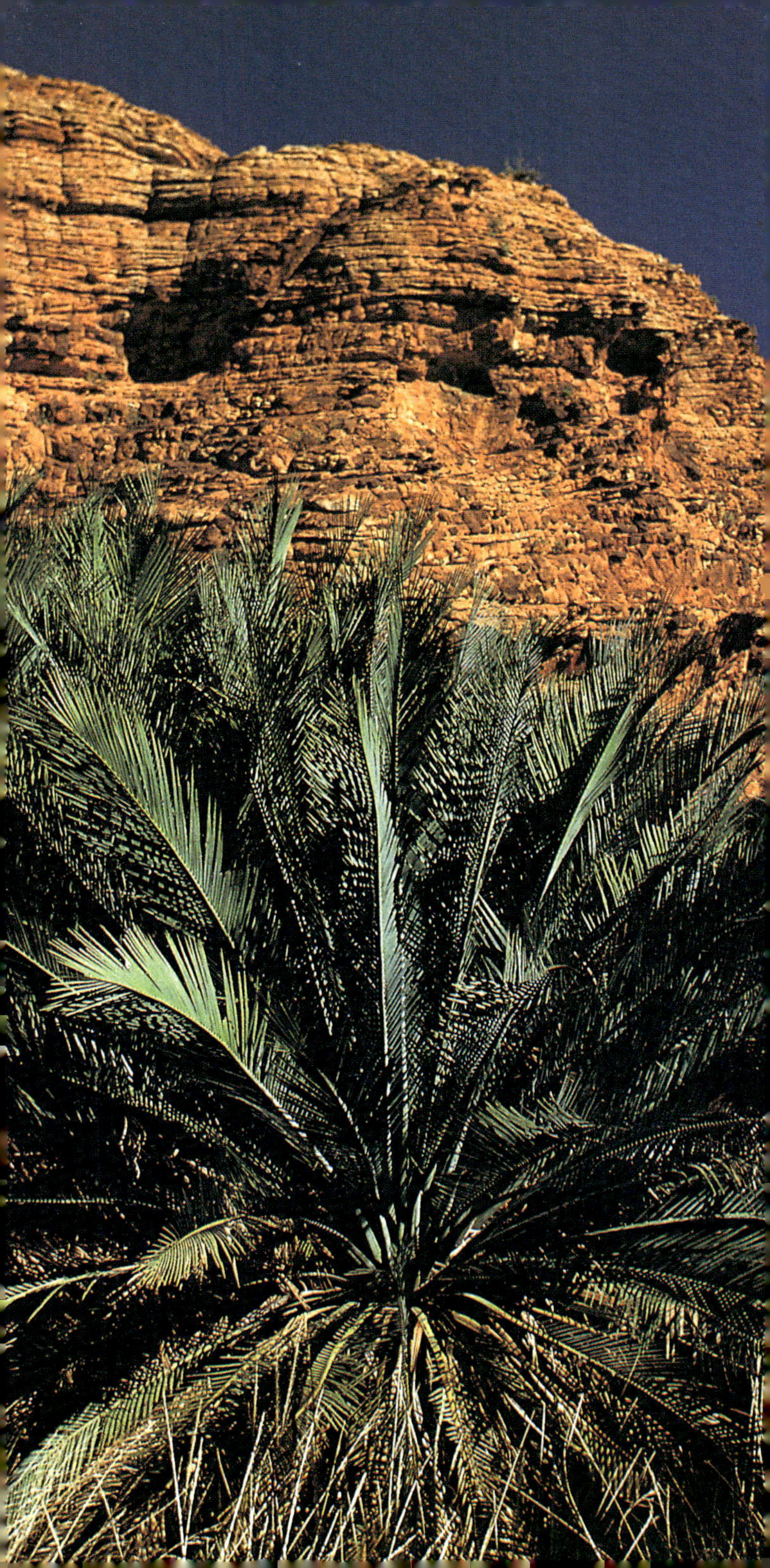

INDEX

Italic page numbers refer to illustrations

A*belmoschus moschatus* 21, *21*
Ablennes hians 52
Acacia spp. 65, 129
  A. aneura 68, *93,* 93–4, *94*
  A. coriacea 135, *135*
  A. kempeana 93, 136, 138, *138,* 140, *140*
  A. victoriae 129
Acanthopagus spp.
  A. australis 53
  A. berda 52
  A. butcheri 53
Acmena spp. 79–80
acul 118, *118*
Adansonia gregorii 10, *11*
Agrotis infusa 13, 13–14
albaraji 25
Albula vulpes 52
Alexander palm 9
allocasuarina 65
Amorphophallus glabra 146–7
Ampelocissus spp.
  A. acetosa 131–2, *132*
  A. gardinera 131–2
Anadara aliena 118, *118*
ants
  green 63, *63*
  honey 66–7, *67*
Apiomorpha pomiformis 67–8
apple
  cocky 29, *29*
  desert 68
  lady 79
  wild red 134, *134*
apple berry 9, *9, 10*

Araucaria bidwillii 16–20, *17, 18–19*
Argyrosomus hololopidotus 52, 53
armeg 118, *118*
armgrass millet 58
arrani 118, *118*
Arripis spp.
  A. georgianus 53
  A. trutta 53
arrowroot
  native 101
  wild 130
Astrelba pectinata 88–9
Atriplex nummularia 101
Australian salmon 53

B*alad* 28, *28*
balk-balk 107, *107*
ballat 28, *28*
ballee 28, *28*
banana, desert *37,* 37–8, *38*
bandicoots 74, 110
Banksia spp.
  B. dentata 98
  B. marginata 98
baobab nut 10, *11*
barnggiti 120
barracuda 52
barramundi 52
Batissa violacea 91–2, 118, *118*
bats, fruit *see* flying foxes
bees 120–1
beverages, fermented 46

Bidyanus bidyanus 53
bilbies 69
Billardiera scandens 9, *9, 10*
birds 54–5
black bean 10–11
blackboy 58–62
black bream 53
blackfish 53
black fruit 12
black kurrajong 76, 78
black-lipped oyster 103
black nerites 12, *12*
bloodwood galls 67, *68*
blue catfish 52
blurter 53
boab tree 10, *11*
Boerhavia diffusa 31
Bogong moths *13,* 13–14
bonefish 52
boomerangs 55
bottlebrush 96
Brachiaria spp. 58
　B. miliiformis 58
Brachychiton spp.
　B. gregorii 76, 78
　B. paradoxum 76–8, *77*
　B. populneum 76, 78
bracken fern 14
bread *see* damper
bream 52, 53
brolgas 55
Bruguiera gymnorrhiza 80–2, *81*
Buchanania obovata 132
buffalo 69
bully 52
bulmurrk 9
bulrush 14–16, *15*
bunya pine 16–20, *17, 18–19, 32*

Burdekin plum 20
burpa 126
Burrawang nuts 20–1
burukpili 89
bush carrot 21, *21*
bush cashew nut 23
bush onions 23–4, *24*
bush potato 24, *25*
bush tomatoes 25–7, *27*

Cabbage tree palm 104
Caladenia spp. 101
Capparis mitchellii 131, *131*
Caranx spp. 52, 53
　C. ignobilis 52
Caretta caretta 85
Carissa lanceolata 76
carrot, bush 21, *21*
cashew nut, bush 23
Cassytha melantha 39, *39, 40*
Castanospermum australe 10–11
catfish 52, 53, *53*
cheese fruit 89–90, *90*
Cheilinus undulatus 52
Chelodina spp. 124
Chelonia spp.
　C. depressa 85
　C. mydas 85
Cherax spp. 140, *141*
cherry ballart *27,* 28
chestnut
　Moreton Bay 10–11, *17*
　water 119
chopper 53
Chrysophrys auratus 53
Clerodendrum floribundum 31
cluster figs *47,* 49
cocky apple 29, *29*

coconut, wild 68
congol 82, *83*, 118, *118*
Conus figulinus 118, *118*
convolvulus 30, *30*
  grass-leaved 30
coral cod 52
coral tree 31
coral trout 52
corkwood 98
Cossidae spp. 136–8
crabs
  hermit 74
  mud *90*, 90–1
Cryptostylis spp. 101
cup-mari 81
Cyathea spp. 121–2
cycads 20–1, 31–6, *32, 34–5, 148–9*
Cycas armstrongii 31–6, *32*
cycasin 33
Cymbidium canaliculatum 101, *102*
Cyperus bulbosus 23–4, *24*

D*abum-dabum* 132
damper, desert seed 38
Davidsonia pruriens 37
Davidson's plum *22*, 37
Dawson River salmon 52
desert apples 68
desert banana *37*, 37–8, *38*
desert fig 47, *48*, 49
desert kurrajong 76, 78
desert raisin 25–7, *27*
devil's twine 39
dhalpi 104
dhangi 29
dhapul 85
dhatum 126

dhuwa bees 120
diamond-scaled mullet 52
Dicksonia antarctica 121–2
Dioscorea spp. 142–5
  D. bulbifera 145, *145*
  D. transversa 143–4
Dipodium spp. 101
Diuris spp. 101
djilka 123, *123*
dodder laurel 39, *39, 40*
dolphins 85
Donax cuneatus 118, *118*
drangol 12, *12*, 118, *118*
drinks, fermented 46
Duboisia hopwoodii 42
ducks 54–5
dugongs 85
dusky flathead 53

E*chidnas* 110
eel tail catfish 52
Egagrostis spp. 58
eggs
  emu 42
  goose 55
  turtle *123*, 124
Eleocharis dulcis 119
Eleutheronema tetradactylum 52
emu berry 41, *41*
emus 42–3, *43, 44–5*, 74
emu tucker 104
Entada phaseoloides 81, 85, 88, *88*
Epinephelus spp. 52
Eretmochelys imbricata 85
Erythrina vespertilio 31
Eucalyptus terminalis 67–8
euros 75

evite 118, *118*
Exocarpus spp.
   E. cupressiformis 28, *28*
   E. latifolius 27

F*icus* spp. 47–9
   F. opposita 47
   F. platypoda 47, *48*, 49
   F. racemosa var. *glomerata* 49
   F. superba 49
figs 47–9
   cluster *47*, 49
   desert 47, *48*, 49
   Moreton Bay 47
   sand 49
   sandpaper 47
file snakes 49–50, *50*
fish 52–3
flatbacked turtle 85
flat tail 52
flying foxes 50–1, *51*
forktail catfish 52
fruit bats *see* flying foxes
fundul 118, *118*

G*ame*, introduced 69
ganguri 143, 143–4
ganj 119
ganyawu 23
garfish 52
geese 54–5, 74
Geodorum spp. 101
giant perch 52
giant trevally 52
ginger, native 96
gingin 24, *25*
Girella tricuspidata 53
Glossodia spp. 101
goannas 56–7, *56–7*

golden perch 53
grapes, wild 131–2, *132*
grass seed 58, 88–9
grass tree 58–62, *59*, *60–1*, *62*, 96
green ants 63, *63*
green plum 63–4, *64*
green turtle 85
Grevillea spp. 96, *97*
   G. eriostachya 97
   G. pteridifolia 98
Grewia retusifolia 41, *41*
Gronophyllum ramsayi 9
groper 52
grubs 64–5
   witchetty 136–8, *137*
gum 65–6
guninyi 89, *90*

H*akea suberea* 98
hawksbill turtle 85
Hemiramphus spp. 52
herb seeds 58, 107–8
hermit crabs 74
herring 53
Hicksbeachia pinnatifolia 100
honey *see* nectar; sugarbag honey
honey ants 66–7, *67*
Hornstedtia scottiana 96
hunting techniques 74–5
   birds 54–5
   kangaroos 70–1
Hyotissa spp. 103
   H. quirites 118, *118*

I*bis* 54–5
ininti 31
insect galls 67–8, *68*

Ipomoea spp. 30, *30*
 I. brasiliensis 30
 I. costata 142–3
 I. gracilis 30
 I. graminea 30
irkilli 135, *135*
ironwood 65

J
abiru *55, 159*
janmarda 23
jewfish 52, 53
Johnny cakes 38
jungara 29
jungle land snail 70, *70*
jungle snail 118, *118*

K
aanthuc 118, *118*
kampurarpa 25–6, *27*
kanawarangi 146
kangaroos 70–5, *73*
kingfish 52
konkleberry 76
kumbuk 118, *118*
kurrajong 76–8, *77, 78*

L
ady apple 79
Lates calcarifer 52
leathery 52
Leichhardtia australis 31, *37*, 37–8
Lepidochelys olivacea 85
lerps 67
Lethrinus nebulosus 52
lillypilly *22, 79,* 79–80
limbuk 24, *25*
Lioconcha sulcatina 118, *118*
lirrawar 120
Livistona spp.
 L. australis 104
 L. benthamii 104
 L. humilis 104
lizard (fish) 53
lizards 56–7
Liza vaigiensis 52
loggerhead turtle 85
long-necked turtles 124–6, *125*
longtom 52
long yam *142, 143,* 143–4
Lopha folium 103
lowiya 146
luderick 53
Lypernathus spp. 101

M
acadamia *32*
Maccullochella peeli 53
mackerel 52
Macquaria ambigua 53
Macrozamia spp.
 M. communis 20–1
 M. macdonnellii 20
 M. miquelii 20–1
 M. spiralis 20–1
macrozamin 33
mangaitj 46
mangrove 80–2, *81, 82*
 white 129
mangrove snail 82–3, *83*
mangrove worm 83–5
manna 67
manyarr 120
Marcia spp. 109–10
 M. liantina 118, *118*
mardunggudj 132
marrakangalay 21, *21*
Marsilea drummondii 95, *95*
matchbox bean 81, 82, 85, 88, *88*

Melo amphora 118, *118*
Melophus bagoti 66–7
Microstemma spp. 63
Microtis spp. 101
Mieroseris scapigera 146
milnhirri 120
Mitchell grass 88–9
monkey nuts *100*
  red *22*
Moreton Bay chestnut 10–11, *17*
Moreton Bay fig 47
morinda 89–90, *90*
Morinda citrifolia 89–90, *90*
mud crab *90*, 90–1
mud oyster 91–2
Mugil cephalus 52, 53
mukaki 133
mulga 68, *93*, 93–4, *94*
mullet 52, 53
mulloway 52, 53
munydjudj 132
Murray cod 53
murrnong 146
murunga 63

Namiri 120–1
nardoo 95, *95*
narra 120–1
native arrowroot 101
native ginger 96
native raspberry 96, *96*
nectar 96–8
Nelumbo nucifera 113, 116–17
Neoarius australis 52
Nerita lineata 12, *12*, 118, *118*
New Zealand spinach 98

ngaru 25–6
niwuda 120
nonda plum 98–100, *99*, *100*
no'omb 81, *81*
nut-milk 99
nuts 100
  see also names of specific nuts e.g. baobab nut; cycads; kurrajong
nyiri 23–4
Nymphaea spp. 126–9, *127*, *128*

Old man saltbush 101
onions, bush 23–4, *24*
orange, wild desert 131, *131*
orchids 101
Oryza sativa 134
oysters 103
  mud 91–2

Pacific ridley 85
pallert 28, *28*
palm
  Alexander 9
  cabbage tree 104
  see also burrawang nuts; cycads; pandanus
palm heart 104
pandanus 104–6, *105*
Pandanus spiralis 46, 104–6
Panicum spp. 38, 58
panja 119
paperbark *8*, *147*
Parinari nonda 98–100, *99*
peach, wild 132, *133*
peanut tree 107, *107*
pelicans 55
pigface *139*

pigs, wild 69
pigweed 107–8, *108*
pilchard 52
pine, bunya 16–20, *17, 18–19, 32*
pine plum, brown *22*
pipi 118, *118*
pipis 109–10
Planchonia careya 29, *29*
Platycephalus fuscus 53
Plectroploma maculatum 52
Pleiogynium timorense 20
plums
    Burdekin 20
    Davidson's 37
    green 63–4, *64*
    nonda *99*, 99–100, *100*
    wild 132–3
poisonous plants 11, 33, 36, 42, 76–8, 85, 88
Polymesoda coaxans 90–1
Pomatomus saltatrix 53
Portulaca spp. 38
    P. intraterranea 107–8
    P. oleracea 107–8, *108*
possums 110
potato, bush 24, *25*
Prasophyllum spp. 101
Pristis zijsron 52
Prostanthera striatiflora 42
Pteridum esculentum 14
Pterostylis spp. 101

Quandong *32*, 110–13, *111, 112*
queenfish 52
quince, wild 29, *29*

Rabbits 69

raisin, desert 25–7, *27*
rakay 119
raspberry, native 96, *96*
red bream 53
red kurrajong 76–8, *77*
reptiles 56–7
    see also file snakes; turtles
rice, wild 134
rock cod 52
rock orchid *101*
round yam 145, *145*
Rubus parviflorus 96, *96*

Saccostrea tuberculata 103
sacred lotus 113, *114–17*
salmon 52, 53
saltbush, old man 101
sandalwood 133
sandfig 49
sand mullet 52
sandpaper fig 47
Santalum spp.
    S. acuminatum 110–13, *112*
    S. lanceolatum 132–3
saratoga 52
sardine 52
Sardinops neopilchardus 52
sawfish 52
sawshark 52
Scleropages leichhardtii 52
Scomberoides lysan 52
Scomberomorus commersoni 52
Scylla serrata 90–1
sea pike 52
seeds 38
    grass 58, 88–9
    herb 58, 107–8
    wattle 93–4, 129, 140
Semicarpus australiensis 23

shark 52
shellfish 12, 82–5, 91–2, 103, *109,* 109–10, *110,* 118, *118*
shipworms 83–5, *84*
silver bream 53
silver perch 53
snail, jungle land 70, *70*
snakes 57
  file 49–50, *50*
snapper 52, 53
Solanum spp. 25–7, *27*
  S. centrale 25–6, *27*
  S. chippendalei 25, *27*
  S. cleistogamum 25
  S. ellipticum 25
  S. esuriale 25, 26
  S. petrophilum 25–6
spangled emperor 52
Sphyraena barracuda 52
spike rush 119
spinach, New Zealand 98
spoonbills, yellow-billed *54*
squire 53
Sterculia quadrifida 107, *107*
sugarbag honey 120–1, *121*
sugar bread *68*
sultana, bush 25
Syzygium spp. *79,* 79–80, 134, *134*
  S. suborbiculare 79

T*acca leontopetaloides* 130
tailor 53
Tandanus tandanus 52, 53
Telescopium telescopium 82–3, *83*
Terebralia palustris 82–3, 118, *118*

Teredo spp. 83–5
Terminalia spp.
  T. carpentariae 132, *133*
  T. ferdinandiana 63–4, *64*
  T. melanocarpa 12
  T. muellii 12
Tetragonia tetragonoides 98
th'arr 118, *118*
Thelymitra 101
threadfin salmon 52
tomatoes, bush 25–7, *27*
Tommy ruff 53
toxins *see* poisonous plants
tree fern 121–2, *122*
tree orchid 101, *102*
trevally 52, 53
Trisidos yongei 118, *118*
tubers, desert 24, 31
turtles 122–6
  sea 85
Typha spp. 14–16, *15*

V*igna lanceolata* 24, *25*

W*akati* 38
wak wak 126
wallabies 75
wama 94
wanakidji 25
wanangka 120–1
wanari 94
wangunu 58
water buffalo 69
water chestnut 119
waterlily 126–9, *127, 128*
wattle, wiry 135, *135, 136*
wattle gum 65
wattle seed 93–4, 129, 140
whales 85

whitefish 52
wijirrki 47, 49
wild arrowroot 130
wild coconut 68
wild desert orange 131, *131*
wild grapes 131–2, *132*
wild peach 132, *133*
wild plum 132–3
wild quince 29, *29*
wild red apple 134, *134*
wild rice 134
wintalka 140
wiry wattle 135, *135, 136*
witchetty bush 93, 136–7, 138, *138*, 140, *140*
witchetty grubs 136–8, *137*
woolybutt grass 58

X*anthomelon pachystylum* 70, 118, *118*

Xanthorrhoea spp. 46
  X. australis 58–62, *59, 62*

Y abbies 140, *141*
yakajiri 25
yala 142
yam daisy 146
yams 24, 142–5
  yellow lily 146–7
yarrpany bees 120
yelka 23–4, *24*
yellow belly 53
yellow fruit 25
yellow lily yam 146–7
yipirntiri 25
yirritja bees 120

Z amia palm nuts 20–1, *21*
zamia staggers 21, 33

Opposite: Black-necked stork or jabiru from Northern Australia.
PHOTO: LEO MEIER